James Harvey

Paper money

The money of civilization

James Harvey

Paper money
The money of civilization

ISBN/EAN: 9783744723329

Printed in Europe, USA, Canada, Australia, Japan

Cover: Foto ©Suzi / pixelio.de

More available books at **www.hansebooks.com**

PAPER MONEY,

THE MONEY OF CIVILIZATION. AN ISSUE BY THE STATE, AND A LEGAL TENDER IN PAYMENT OF TAXES.

By JAMES HARVEY,

LIVERPOOL.

"The intricacy of the question has been much increased by the hitherto necessary use of marketable commodities, such as gold, silver, salt, shells, etc., to give intrinsic value and security to money; but the final and best definition, is, that it is a documentary promise, ratified and guaranteed by the nation, to give or find a certain quantity of labour or the results of labour."—*John Ruskin.*

"Whether, in the rude original of society, the first step was not the exchange of commodities; the next, the substitution of metals by weight as the common medium of circulation; after this, the making use of coin; lastly, a further refinement by the use of paper with proper marks and signatures? And whether this, as it is the last, is not also the greatest improvement?"—*Bishop Berkely's "Querist."*

LONDON:

PROVOST & CO., 36, HENRIETTA ST., COVENT GARDEN.

1877.

PREFACE.

THE advocacy of Paper Money has been so effectually silenced in this country, that the very mention of it opens either a storm of angry invective, or an out-pour of ridicule, whilst its advocates have hitherto confined themselves to putting forth their views in pamphlets and broad-sheets.

The Author has published this book that the future inquirer may find collected together the various authorities who have advocated this unpopular subject, and in a form that will enable it to be shelved and catalogued in the various libraries to which it will be presented, including the library of the British Museum. The writer feels sure that at some future time all thinking men will read with interest these pages, where the author's opinions are enforced by such writers as Bishop Berkely, John Locke, Roger North, Andrew Yarranton, Edward Capps, John Taylor, John Ruskin, Louis Blanc, and Jonathan Duncan, and last not least, Sir John Sinclair, whose counsels prompted Mr. Pitt to try a new system of finance,—a system resorted to through stern necessity, and perhaps somewhat empirically, but which proved the weapon by which the foreign invader was repelled, and ultimately driven into exile; but at the same time wonderfully stimulating internal trade. The first name in the list of writers is Bishop Berkely. His celebrated "Querist" laid down correct principles seventy years before Adam Smith, who touched on the subject in an obscure and contradictory manner, indicating a timid repugnance to forego gold as a basis. Especial reference is made to the proposal for Consol notes, as proposed by the

Liverpool Currency Reform Association.   Attention is also called to the extracts from Bishop Berkely's "Querist," where the Socratic system of interrogation is resorted to, as being less dictatorial and less offensive to minds deeply infected with prejudice and that self-love which prompts most men to look upon their opinions as a sort of private property, not to be disturbed or interfered with.

It requires faith in the power of truth to attempt to stem this worship of gold, which Sir John Sinclair truly describes as a delirium and an infatuation.

JAMES HARVEY.

CHATHAM PLACE, LIVERPOOL.

INDEX.

APPENDIX.

PAPER MONEY,

THE MONEY OF CIVILIZATION.

CHAPTER I.

SIR ROBERT PEEL'S BILL.

" The landlords enacted a corn law to make corn dear, and passed Peel's Bill to make corn cheap."

" ALL civilized nations enact certain fundamental laws. These are governing powers, and subsequent laws are intended to carry them out into practical use. The most important fundamental law in any nation is that which institutes MONEY; for money governs the distribution of property, and thus affects in a thousand ways the relations of man to man. If wrongly instituted, it cannot be rightly governed by any subsequent laws; and the wrong distribution of property consequent upon it must corrupt society in all its branches. The evils engendered can never be remedied except by altering the fundamental law. Changes in the subsequent laws, so long as they are founded on a wrong base, can only result in the exchange of one evil for another. The proposition that wrong premises will produce wrong conclusions is often stated,

1

yet it is seldom fully understood and properly appreciated. A simple illustration will show the governing power of a fundamental principle. A good house cannot be built except upon a good foundation. The mason-work above may be laid of the best material and by the best workmen; but if the foundation be not sound, and sink at each corner from five to twenty inches, although the house should not fall, yet this movement of the foundation will distort the floors, ceilings, roof, and rooms from their proper shape; and no propping or patching up of floors, ceilings, roof, or rooms will ever make the house a good one.

The rights of property.

One of the chief objects for which Governments are instituted is to insure the protection of the rights of property. The security of these rights is essential to the welfare of the people. Their infringement is the cause of nearly all legal procedures. Such crimes as theft, gambling, fraud in business, bribery in courts of law, etc., which consist in unjustly obtaining property without rendering an equivalent, are violations of the rights of property.

The most sacred right of property is that of a man in the products of his own labour. It is to labour we are indebted for all the necessaries, comforts, and luxuries of life. The exaction of usury for the use of an instrument for exchanging the products of that labour is, therefore, the greatest violation of that right.

Sir Robert Peel's exordium.

In entering upon the great controversy of Paper against Gold, no fitter introduction can be found than the eloquent exordium with which Sir Robert Peel commenced his speech in bringing forward his celebrated Bill of 1844, in which he describes the importance of this inquiry :—

" There is no contract, public or private, no engagement, national or individual, which is unaffected by it. The enterprises of commerce, the profits of trade, the arrangements to be made in all the domestic concerns of life, the wages of labour, the transactions of the highest and of the lowest amount, the payment of the national debt, the provision for the national expenditure on the one hand, and the command which the coin of the lowest denomination has over the necessaries of life on the other, are all affected by the decision to which we may come on the great question which I am about to introduce to the consideration of the committee."

In 1817, a quarter of a century before this speech was delivered, Sir Robert Peel had deserted the financial policy of Mr. Pitt, and had given in his adhesion to the opposite theory. This unfortunate decision inflicted on this country indescribable calamities. No foreign invasion could have affected all ranks so disastrously as the sudden introduction of this rash, ill-advised, and pedantic measure, acting so energetically as it did, on price. " Each succeeding year since the war," said Mr. Tierney, " made things worse. The distress, at first confined principally to our agriculture, has spread to every branch of trade and industry, and the national misery has reached a point wholly without precedent since the Norman Conquest."

Mr. Matthias Attwood thus described the effects of this

Disastrous effects of Sir Robert Peel's Bill.

measure : " The Act fell on the calm prosperity of the people, on the prosperous industry of the country—to confound, disorder, and destroy. All the calamities of 1816 were renewed. The blow was first felt by the manufacturing population. Without employment, without food, they prepared for resistance ; and the spirit was so hostile that the speech from the throne accused them of aiming at the subversion of the rights of property and of all order in society, and the overthrow of the political institutions of the country."

Popular feeling in favour of gold.
Sir J. Sinclair : see p. 29.

The return to cash payments was easily effected, chiming in as it did with popular prejudice. Men of all parties were for once unanimous. Mr. Horner, the principal advocate for a change, was allowed to nominate a committee of his own friends; all ingenious but speculative men, chiefly consisting of the Whig party, who, by a long banishment from office, had lost all practical acquaintance with affairs. The leaders of the people, Mr. Cobbett and Mr. Hunt, and others,* attributed all the distress to the one-pound notes. Last of all, under the delirium of the day, the periodical and daily press seconded the popular enthusiasm. Reviews, magazines, and journals were beginning to exercise that

The Press also.
Adm. Maxse: App. A.

* Thomas Payne wrote a book entitled the " Downfall of Pitt's Finance," in which he avers that " of all the varieties of base coin, paper money is the basest. It has the least intrinsic value of anything that can be put in the place of gold and silver. A hobnail or a piece of wampum far exceeds it, and there would be more propriety in making these articles legal tender than to make paper so."

William Cobbett maintained that " if any man were permitted to write a ' promise to pay ' on the crown of his hat, it would require no prophet to foretell that the country would be inundated " !

influence on the public mind which they have retained to this day; but being conducted by theorists and literary men unacquainted with affairs, they have too readily encouraged the popular delusion; and, moreover, the daily newspapers, being mercantile speculations in the hands of capitalists, have systematically upheld what they conceive to be their interests—unreasonably supposed to be bound up with the newly-introduced system. In fact, to have taken an opposite course would have damaged their popularity with their readers. So much is this the case, and so utterly has the advocacy been extinguished, that Professor Bonamy Price, of Oxford, is enabled to assert, in his "Principles of Currency," that "the defence of an inconvertible currency may be said to have disappeared from English literature. No public writer of any weight, for years past, has committed himself to so hopeless a cause. On the Continent, inconvertible currencies still linger in some States; but they are not defended *on the ground of principle*—they are excused, on the plea of an overwhelming necessity. The nations who adopt them are the objects of a certain pity, as the victims of a misfortune which vanquishes their judgment." And in this somewhat supercilious verdict his brother professors would doubtless concur. But it has always been so; and it was in this class that Galileo found his most inveterate opponents. Nevertheless, the "*ground of principle*" is going to be taken, and "the object of a certain pity" may perhaps be discovered where the Professor might least expect him.

Bonamy Price.

America taking up the ques- iton. The defence of a representative paper money is not so hopeless a matter, if the Professor will look across the Atlantic, where he will find the " soft-money " advocates are gaining strength, have begun an organized agitation, have succeeded in making it a hustings question, and have even had sufficient influence to get Governor Hendricks nominated as Vice-President. The chances of immediate success in that contest may be small; but when the people are instructed, and their eyes opened to the cause of their misfortunes, reform is not far off. This agitation and discussion in America must react on this country, and this inveterate tabooing of a vital question in the House of Commons must come to an end.

The Fund- ing system The Funding system, a system which compels all debtor nations to pay annual interest in gold, is showing signs of breaking up. The *Times* confessed the other day that there were only four States which could be considered solvent. Indebtedness is paralyzing the industry of all nations. This must attract the attention it deserves; and the time is approaching, slowly but surely, when national debts will be closely investigated, and their obligations questioned.

In spite of the dictum of the *Times*, which the commercial world still persists in receiving with implicit faith; in spite of the hostility of the press; in spite of the reticence of the House of Commons, the time must come when public attention will inevitably be drawn to the inquiry, " Is money to be composed of the dearest metal known, or is it to be a documentary instrument of exchange to be issued by the State ? "

There are three theories.

The first is, that money must have intrinsic value, and that as intrinsic value is concentrated in gold, thereby making transmission easy, gold is the proper commodity (it may be here conceded that if it is to be a commodity and to have intrinsic value, gold is the best); that, duly weighed, essayed, and coined by the Mint, under the supervision of the State, it shall have conferred on it by Act of Parliament a money denomination; that in this country the weight of five pennyweights and three grains shall be the weight of the sovereign, and that such coin shall be legal tender for twenty shillings of taxes, and consequently of debts, and that for convenience and to obviate the difficulty of carriage to and fro of large sums, a certificate of gold in the form of a bank-note shall be issued. *First theory.*

The second theory is, that gold alone shall be money, and that all paper should be abolished. This is the theory of a savage, and being impracticable in a civilized community, has few advocates. *Second theory.*

The third theory, and the one practically carried out by Sir Robert Peel's Bill, is, that though the note carries on its face a " promise to pay gold," yet the necessities of trade require that there shall be more notes, or " promises to pay," than there is gold in the Treasury to honour them if presented. *Third theory.*

If one commodity cannot possibly be legal tender for all

other commodities, then these propositions are deemed by the advocates of documentary money totally untenable. They maintain that money, as representative of value and as the exponent of price, must, like a warehouse warrant, or a bill of lading, or even a postage stamp, be documentary, and that consequently paper as a material must be the best.

Exchequer note : See App.

This paper document must declare on the face of it that it is issued by the State, and that it is legal tender for debts and taxes; the amount of issue to be fixed by Parliament. It is evident that this does away with the formula we are all familiar with, "I promise to pay."

Supposed difficulty of the question.

The difficulty which has generally been supposed to envelop the whole question must account for the universal indisposition to look into it. A subject so important, however, as that which regulates every bargain made between man and man, cannot be neglected with impunity. Sir Robert has told us there is no contract, public or private, no engagement, national or individual, which is unaffected by it. Earlier in 1825 Sir James Graham had said, "The real difficulties of the State, and the present danger of the landed interest, will be found to lurk under the question of currency." This was said fifty years since, and the real difficulties of the State still lurk under it; and the purport of these pages is to drag those hidden dangers forth, to show that it lies at the root of the deplorable contest between labour and capital, and of that wide separation which is taking place between the propertied and the unpropertied classes.

Last, not least, to a vicious monetary system we owe that Effort required to overcome prejudice. rapid growth of usury which is prostrating industry and destroying the happiness and comfort of the people. If, then, the interests of all classes are compromised, surely the English people will, under the direction of the leading intellects of the day, master the plain principle indicated above. But as there is no "royal road to learning" of any kind, so there is no possibility of understanding this question without some attention, thought, and investigation. It certainly does require a vigorous mental effort to overcome the prejudices instilled into us from infancy, prejudices imbibed in the nursery tale, strengthened in the school, inculcated in history, and fostered by the periodical and the newspaper of the day. Against us, wealth, talent, and political influence, and, more to be dreaded, the writers of established reputation,—John Stuart Mill, Jeremy Bentham, Lord Overstone, Bonamy Price, Professor Fawcett, Dr. W. B. Hodgson, and all political economists excepting John Ruskin. Even Thomas Carlyle has never applied his powerful mind to its consideration, confining himself chiefly to denunciations and jeremiads. One consolation remains. Truth, which recom- True principles will prevail. mends itself to the hearts and consciences of all men, will prevail; from the beginning of the world it has been slowly, but surely, forcing its way, obtaining from age to age increased and increasing numbers of worshippers. It seems, however, as though error in all its phases must be tried by mankind, and not until all its Proteus forms have been exhausted can truth be permanently established. This is ably set forth by Sir Charles Lyell in his history of the struggles of geology through every fantastic variety of error, till at last true theories were laid down never to be shaken. One source of hope lies in the fact that leading men among the working classes are bringing their intellectual influence to bear on those less advanced, whilst the prominence given to these views in the present Presidential election in America indicates progress.

This rash and daring monetary revolution took place on the close of the wars with Napoleon. It is necessary to give a rapid sketch of its introduction and consequences.

Cash pay ments in- troduced at the peace.

The war came to an end, and the nation justly expected that the prosperity and happiness of the community would make more progress in a time of peace. But during the war, two causes had been operating on the nation's welfare. There was the war exhausting the resources of the country and making it poor; and there was an adequate paper currency developing the energies of the country and making it rich. We had vanquished our enemy, and secured for the country, as was fondly believed, the blessings of peace. The very next step was, to turn our back upon our friend Pitt's monetary system, and deprive peace of its blessings. Immediately after the proclamation of peace, the Bank of England received an intimation that it must prepare for a return to cash payments. It contracted its issues accord-

Introduc- tion of Peel's Bill and conse- quences.

ingly. "Such a scene," says Sir James Graham, "both of agricultural and commercial distress, ensued as this unhappy country, till that time, had never witnessed." The Govern-

ment was dismayed at the suffering which this merely con-
templated measure had produced. In their distress the farmers
fondly looked to the time of high prices, for as this had
been coincident with a time of war, they illogically deemed
the war to be the cause of their prosperity, and not the
paper money circulating at the time. The circulating
medium was again increased, and by 1819 all the interests
of the country were in a prosperous condition. Again
Peel's Bill became the law of the land, and in a few months
the severest distress pervaded all classes. Again the Government of the day relented. In 1822 a small-note Act was
passed, and one-pound notes put into circulation. The
country recovered rapidly, and the revenue so increased
that the Chancellor of the Exchequer acquired the name of
"Prosperity Robinson." But it became advantageous to
export gold; the circulation was contracted, the dogma of
the convertibility of the note making it imperative on the
Bank to cancel notes as the gold decreased. This caused
the panic of 1825, with its ruinous consequences. The blow
fell first on the bankers. One-eighth of the country bankers Bankers
stop
in England and six of the London banks stopped payment. payment.
They were told "that they deserved their ruin,—it arose
from an over-issue of notes"; that over-issue which, if it
existed, the Government had done everything to encourage.
The traders and manufacturers of the country speedily felt
the ill effects of the panic of 1825. They were told that
their sufferings arose from an over-production of commodities. They had worked too hard, risen too early, been too

ingenious in increasing the produce of their industry. " Yet the poor in the manufacturing districts were starving with food in abundance staring them in their face," said Mr. Francis, and two hundred families were officially declared to have among them only four blankets.

Cotton famine.

This was a state of things again exemplified in the cotton famine. This was not a famine of food, clothes, lodging, furniture, or fuel; and yet the starving factory population passed every day the doors of warehouses and stores full of all these necessaries. A paper issued on their labour, productively exercised, say, on transferring heavy clay to light soils, on carrying the alluvium of river valleys back to the hill sides, on conveying the lime of Derbyshire on cheap railways made by themselves, on embanking and warping the estuaries of the Lune, the Ribble, the Mersey, and the Dee, and lastly on improving their towns—such labour, so productively exercised, would have found them in wages, and consequently in food, lodging, clothes, furni-

State of towns : App. B.

ture, and fuel. With regard to the last item, the improvement of their towns, the obvious utility of this will be made evident by the description which appeared in the *Times* of the state of those small cottages which either the factory owner himself or some needy speculative builder runs up in squalid and monotonous uniformity in the vicinity of the works.

Reform agitation.

To recur again to the continuous narrative. In 1829 and 1830 the agricultural distress was again extreme, whilst petitions poured in from every part of the country and from all interests,—petitions which cannot now be read without shrinking from the details of misery which they record. These sufferings created political discontent, which culminated in the Reform agitation. Popular feeling was roused to such a degree that the Ministers thought it advisable to dissuade the King (William IV.) from attending the City banquet. A placard was extensively posted on the walls of London—" Stop the Duke!—Go for gold!" These significant words indicated that some minds had guessed the real cause of this dreadful state of things. An extract from Mr. Francis's "History of the Bank of England" describes the excitement :—

Mr. Francis : Extract.

" The knowledge that the great opponent of the Bill, the Duke of Wellington, was likely to be recalled to power, spread throughout the Metropolis. Staves with the tri-coloured devices painted on them, and sticks with concealed swords, were sold in great quantities ; while the demand for bludgeons could scarcely be supplied. A speaker of the Birminghan Political Union, amid the shouts of assembled multitudes, called on his hearers to pay no taxes till the Bill was passed ; while a forest of hands sprang up in answer to his solemn but misguided appeal. A terrible excitement was exhibited throughout England. Preparations were made for a great tragedy. Warrants were prepared. The leaders of political unions were to be apprehended. Troops began to march on disaffected places. The monetary interest felt the shock. On every wall throughout the Metropolis the significant words " Stop the Duke !—Go for

gold!" were boldly placarded. For a week the Corporation
sustained a run upon its specie, which was reduced to
£5,000,000. In one day £300,000 were paid. It soon became questionable whether the run for gold would not drain
every banker in the kingdom; and the writing on the wall
spoke to those having authority with a power far exceeding
the most brilliant oratory. Lord Lyndhurst found it impossible to form a Ministry, and Earl Grey was recalled.
That the demand was political was proved by the trifling
nature of the applications from the country bankers. ' I
never saw the hall of the Bank,' said Mr. Richards in his
evidence in 1832, 'except in 1825, so crowded with appli-
cants tendering their notes.' They had not in general the
appearance of people from the country. One person, who
had money with Jones Loyd & Co. to the amount of
£20,000, drew it from them in the form of notes, and then
went to the bank and demanded gold;" evidence enough
from the above extract of the dangers to which Sir R. Peel's
Gold Bill subjects the Government. If the holders of the
savings banks were to combine under any excitement, they
alone could break the Bank, and scotch the wheels of
Government. These new banks seem oblivious of the fact
that they are under Peel's Bill, and that they are exposed to
a run for gold by their depositors, who have been well
described as "a mine of panic ready to explode under their
feet at any moment."

The Reform Bill brought no relief, its real and only
operation being to destroy the landlord's monopoly of the

representation of the people, and to admit more manufacturers, merchants, bankers, and capitalists into the House
of Commons. Not a voice was raised in this reformed
House of Commons on the subject. In 1837, another
panic, and in 1839 the Bank had to borrow two and a half
millions from the Bank of France to escape bankruptcy.
This disgraceful loan induced the House of Commons to
appoint a committee, before which Mr Cobden gave
evidence.

Bark of
England
borrows
2½ millions
from the
Bank of
France:
C.App.

CHAPTER II.

" It was a great discovery when a metallic medium was substituted for
barter ; it was also a great discovery when paper was made convertible into
gold and silver ; but a third discovery was reserved for our own times
namely, that with an inconvertible paper currency, agriculture, commerce
and manufactures, might advance in a career of unexampled prosperity."—
SIR JOHN SINCLAIR.

IN 1843 the Government propounded the doctrine "that
indirect taxation had reached its limits." The Whig

Whig party resign.

party began rapidly to lose that popularity which they had
acquired by their bold measure of parliamentary reform.
The Conservatives came into power, and Sir Robert Peel, to
cover the deficit of ten millions left by the Whigs—a deficit
the result of bad money laws—imposed the Income Tax. In

Sir Robert introduces the Bill of 1844.

1844 Sir Robert Peel introduced the Bank Charter Act, in
doing which he said that "during the last twenty years
four decisive proofs, at four distinct periods, had been given,
namely, in 1825, 1832, 1837, and 1839, that under the present system " (a system of his own devising) " the principle
of convertibility had been endangered." This was the condemnation of his favourite Bill,—a Bill which he fondly
anticipated would establish his fame as a financier for ever,
but whose disastrous operation he only aggravated, as

as proved by the panic of 1847, which followed his amendment of 1844, whilst in the space of ten years ninety banks broke, with liabilities of forty-seven millions. This, the matured wisdom of bullionism, Mr. Goulborne called " a perfect system."

In October 1847 came another dreadful panic, in which *Panic, 1847.* the Bank was only saved from stopping payment by the interference of the Government; Lord John Russell being Prime Minister. This was remarkable as, occurring directly after the inauguration of the Free Trade system, indicating clearly that Free Trade was not the end-all and cure-all of all commercial calamities, but that the source of evil lay elsewhere. The interference of the Government *Minister's letter.* consisted in the Minister writing a letter, suspending the Act passed three years before, and allowing the Bank to issue inconvertible paper, though at the same time everybody else was forced to pay in gold; so that in effect any debtor to the Bank was compelled to pay in gold, but all the creditors of the Bank might be paid in paper.

It was at this time that the merchants of Liverpool pre- *Memorial of merchants of Liverpool : App. D.* sented their memorial representing the distress they were in, and begging for advances on the credit of the country ; in other words, for an issue of Exchequer Notes.

In 1857 another panic took place. In ten years, which *Panic of 1857.* seems to be the interval established between these commercial storms, occurred the Gurney panic, this in 1866, so-called from the failure of that great discounting house,—a failure which spread consternation throughout the kingdom. This

2

event showed plainly that the unexpected and extraordinary discoveries of gold in Australia and California could not in the least lessen the liability to panic. That the discoveries did for a time stimulate trade and confer temporary prosperity. on the country is true enough. The country was gasping for more money, and more money came. To Rector Twells we owe this rapid sketch of the operation of " this great experiment," as Lord Ashburton called it, an experiment condemned by the very test Lord Overstone would judge it by, " that of affording every possible security for the effectual maintenance of specie payments." This failure under trial may be made plain by the following returns of the Bank of England on the weeks in October 1847 and 1857 :—

In October, 1847.

Liabilities :—Notes or promises to pay sovereigns . . . . 34 millions.

Assets :—Gold in the Issue departments. . 8 ,,

Balance which the Bank could not pay in gold . . . . 26 ,,

In October, 1857.

Liabilities :—Notes or promises to pay sovereigns . . . . . . 39 millions.

Assets :—Gold in the issue departments. . 7 ,,

Balance which the Bank could not pay in gold . . . . 32 ,,

It will be seen, not only from the arguments which have been used, but from facts and figures, that this "fair-weather" Bank Charter Act has on two separate occasions, when its true object, the effectual maintenance of specie payments, has been tested, most completely and disgracefully failed. It is impossible to convert the enormous indebtedness of this great nation into gold. The convertibility of the note at a fixed rate has been demonstrated to be a mere political fiction. But there is another and a novel aspect under which this question has recently been presented to the public. The *Times*, the organ of the bullionist party, charges the whole of the people of England with dishonesty. "Any man," it says, "who comes under an engagement to pay a certain sum on a certain given day, pledges himself to deliver so many sovereigns." No doubt, had not the Government letter appeared on Thursday, money would have been worth 20 or 30 per cent., owing to the general panic which would have been created. When we are subsequently told "the hard calculator" sees the time at hand when the gold he has prudently saved will be worth 15 per cent., the Government steps in to frustrate the results of his patient inquiry and reflection. This is the true way of putting the case. In 1857 the mask is thrown off, and the USURER stands revealed.

So it seems the aim of the Bill was, not to supply the people with a sufficiency of money to meet the demands of taxation, state and local, to pay debts and supply the till and the purse, to pay wages and to meet domestic ex-

The *Times* pleads for the "hard calculator."

penses, but to put money in the purse of "hard calculators,"
stock-jobbers, and "watchers of the turn of the market."
Here the Usurer stands revealed in the face of day. It is
not the maintenance of specie payments alone, but such a
maintenance of specie payments as may command an usurious rate of interest which the "hard calculators" require.
Notice the open avowal, the cool adoption of the opprobious
name without a symptom of shame! The *Times* went on,
all candour and ingenuous frankness, with its confessions,
which must have been written by the same Sampson who in
1875 was repudiated and dismissed in an article of withering
rebuke. (Unfortunately, the repudiation and the dismissal
came after an exposure in a court of law.) Not only did the
"hard calculator" calculate on his 20 per cent., but, confessed the *Times*, he expected he should be able also to buy
sugar, silk, and all sorts of articles at a vast reduction.
But his expectations were disappointed, "thanks to the
Government." According to this oracle of the mercantile
world, the producer ought, as a matter of course, to be
sacrificed to the consumer. Put the case of the farmer. A
farmer, in prosperous times, commonly makes the land his
bank,—a fact, be it observed, not entirely lost sight of by
his landlord. Whatever capital he can, by persevering industry and the results of "patient inquiry and reflection,"
accumulate, he invests in the improvement of his land, in
better management, better cultivation of the soil, and the
improvement of his stock. He naturally expects this will
secure to him, if his landlord is not too exacting on the

Sampson
of the
Times.

The case
of the
farmer.

renewal of his lease, the quiet possession of the fruits of his industry. But how mistaken is he in his expectation! There has been another man at work; that is, the "hard calculator." He has improved his understanding of Peel's Bill, and cultivated an acquaintance with the operation of the money market. A monetary crisis comes. Gold goes out of the country; the Bank raises its discounts and reduces the circulation, and the prices of all things fall. And thus the farmer is deprived for years of the fair remuneration for all his industry, and of the interest of the capital which he has invested in the land. The same thing applies to the manufacturer, for he has been building new mills, enlarging his works, extending his trade and employing more hands. Peel's Bill puts a stop to all this. And when the farmer and manufacturer are suffering, and all the country with them, and Government at the eleventh hour steps in to save the country from utter ruin, the usurer complains that prices are not suffered to fall still lower; that he, the consumer, is defrauded of wheat at thirty shillings a quarter, and all other things in proportion; and that he cannot get 20 or 30 per cent. according to his calculation. "Is there among these writers of the *Times* one word of heart-felt regret," wrote that eloquent and indefatigable yet temperate assertor of right principles, the late lamented Rector Twells, "any relenting for the anguish and privations, the broken fortunes and the broken hearts which the Bank Charter Act is at this moment causing? Do they say anything of the distress and poverty of the

The fall of prices affects farmers and manufacturers.

The Times expresses no regret at the distress.

people, thrown by thousands and tens of thousands out of work without any fault of their own? Have they shown the least feeling of commiseration for the working men by whose humble firesides, sufferings, destitution, and starvation are taking up their winter abode? No! Is it so nominated in the bond? Is there one feeling of pity for the victims of this iniquity? No, not one. The whole tenor of their writings is, 'Perish the people of England! but let the hard calculator grasp his 15 per cent.'"

Mr. John Taylor, of the London University, thus puts the question as between the producer and the consumer:— "Cheapness has been cried up as a blessing to the labourer; yet it is difficult to conceive how any one could think that the labourer would be benefited by low prices. A moment's reflection would have served to undeceive him.

Cheapness adds to the purchasing power of the sovereign.

A poor man produces five times as much as he consumes; a rich man consumes (say) five times as much as he produces. Low prices, therefore, are in favour of the rich consumer as five to one, and high prices are in favour of the poor producer as five to one. These numbers are used by way of illustration; it is immaterial what the real proportions are; every one who produces more than he consumes is benefited by high prices more than by low; and every one who lives on property, every one who consumes more than he produces, is benefited by low prices more than high. Yet there are many persons professing to be friends of the labourer, who gravely try to persuade him that low prices are for his special advantage. Having forced down prices by the Currency Acts of 1819 and 1844, they wished the people to believe that low prices are preferable to high prices." This puts the question between the producer and the consumer in a very clear point of view, and it must be remembered that the well-being of the working man is involved in that of the producer.

To illustrate this further. The late rise of prices in the years 1871, 1872, and 1873 had an injurious effect on all living on fixed incomes. Let us take the fund-holder. He went into the market to purchase the necessaries of life, and with the surplus to purchase luxuries. He found all articles doubled in price. His three pounds in the hundred, only brought him in half of what he secured in the period of low prices. What, then, was the effect on the producer? He, with higher wages—for the range of price affected labour—found the market more plentifully supplied by the lessened demand of the fixed income or annuitant class. So great was the change that the butchers in some of the manufacturing towns found that their prime joints were no longer purchased by their former customers in the middle ranks of life, but were monopolised by working men, especially by skilled artizans. The sovereign had lost some of its purchasing power. This, in effect, had lessened the burthen of the national debt, and calculating results, not in money, but in commodities, the burthen of taxation was lightened at least one-third, and in actual operation the debt was reduced from £800,000,000 to £550,000,000, the annual taxation to meet the interest being

[margin notes:] Effect on the fund-holder.

High prices reduce taxation.

reduced from £28,000,000 to £19,000,000 in real burthen, *i.e.*, estimated in food, clothes, lodging, and fuel.

At the time Sir Robert Peel introduced his Bill, the quantity of gold produced year by year hardly sufficed to replace the wear and tear. Its scarcity and the supposed difficulty of adding to its quantity was in his eyes its chief recommendation. Had he lived long enough, however, to see the extraordinary discoveries of California and Australia, he would have been filled with gloomy forebodings, for it was no part of his philosophy to believe that money ought to increase with population and wealth. He would have imagined that the addition of £150,000,000 to our stock of sovereigns, which his Act had made our only money, would disturb the relation of debtor and creditor; especially to the detriment of the latter, always the object of his especial care. The rise of prices would have filled him with dismay, and the relief to the debtor, which is only another word for the workers, would not compensate for the loss to the proper-tied and annuitant classes. The resulting prosperity he would have attributed to free trade.

But this prosperity was soon destroyed. Production, aided by machinery, now extended to agriculture as well as manufactures, soon overtook this additional supply; and the present year, 1876, sees us landed in the old social quag-mire of bad trade, strikes, increasing poverty, and the conse-quent rise of a spirit of discontent. This, with increasing pauperism and the rapid development of a dangerous class, makes the lookout anything but cheerful.

And fixed charges.

Machinery adds to production

A new feature has revealed itself. Though the bullion in the Bank of England stands now (1876) at the unprecedented amount of 34,000,000, trade has not revived, and in this present July, 1876, the rate of discount is only two per cent., because the demand for money is languid. In fact, trade has been so harassed, and the energies of the country so overweighted with rent or the monopoly of land, and with interest of money (the other giant monopoly), the burthen of taxation, state and local, being added, that production in all its branches is rapidly succumbing.   ,

CHAPTER III.

"Some of the best English writers upon commerce set out with observing that the wealth of a country consists, not in its gold and silver only, but in its lands, houses, and consumable goods of all different kinds. In the course of their reasonings, however, the lands, houses, and consumable goods seem to slip out of their memory, and the strain of their argument frequently supposes that all wealth consists in gold and silver, and that to multiply those metals is the great object of national industry and commerce."—ADAM SMITH: *Art.,* "*Mercantile System.*"

Pitt's Bank Restriction Act.

SUCH is a rapid sketch of events in the last fifty years. In direct contrast, let us compare it with Mr. Pitt's system, inaugurated by the celebrated Bank Restriction Act, an Act perhaps empirically resorted to, but whose wonderful action for good showed that a right principle had been hit upon.* And here it will not be out of place to put on record the courage and public spirit of the merchants of London, who met and passed resolutions that they would receive those

* As an indication of the timidity with which Mr. Pitt entered on this experiment, Sir John Sinclair gives the following anecdote :—" Having remitted £70,000 to Manchester and Glasgow on loan before the Exchequer Notes could be prepared, he met Mr. Pitt in the House, who expressed his regret that the pressing wants of those two towns could not be supplied as soon as the occasion demanded. "The money will not be ready for some days," said Mr. Pitt. "It is already gone ; it left London by this evening's mail," was the triumphant answer. Sir John used to add, "Pitt was as much startled as if I had stabbed him."—*Sir John Sinclair's Memoirs*, vol. i., p. 244.

notes in payments. This was the more praiseworthy as, only a short time previously, the French Directory, by their insane and profligate issue of assignats, had thrown discredit on all issues of paper. Sir John Sinclair gives an account of the first Exchequer Notes, the immediate and beneficial effects of which he thus describes :—

"In the year 1793, soon after the commencement of the war, commercial difficulties to an alarming extent began to prevail throughout the country. A general paralysis appeared to seize the country; the number of bankruptcies exceeded all that ever happened in the most calamitous times. An immense number of families were reduced to beggary and ruin. The manufacturers in several of the most flourishing towns were reduced to desperation; several emigrated, numbers enlisted in the army. Panic of 1793.

"The evil to be remedied was a sudden deficiency in the circulating medium. Mr. Pitt proposed a Select Committee of the House of Commons on Commercial Credit, which recommended,—

"That His Majesty should be enabled to direct that Exchequer Bills to the amount of £5,000,000 be laid out for the assistance of such persons as might apply." First issue of Exchequer Notes, 1793.

This recommendation was acted upon.

Those Exchequer Notes gave immediate relief. Seventy thousand pounds were issued, with an actual profit to the nation of four thousand pounds.

The immediate results of this unprecedented innovation on all preconceived notions, this bold leap in the dark, were as

Beneficial
result. extraordinary as unexpected. Trade revived with a sudden
bound, and the country was enabled to put forth all its
energies in the prosecution of the war with France.

Sir John Sinclair, in his Memoirs, gives an animated
description of these results in a speech delivered in the
House of Commons on the 13th May, 1810, when the
Bullion Committee—Mr. Horner, chairman—issued a report
recommending the resumption of cash payments within
two years. It is a significant fact that the publishing of
this Report spread consternation throughout the kingdom ;
banks began everywhere to lessen their issues, panic raised
its terrific head, mercantile credit was shaken, the *Gazette*
was crowded with insolvencies,—all to overthrow results
described as follows :—

Sir J. Sin-
clair on the
beneficial
results. "Perhaps the world never witnessed such a scene as
Great Britain has lately presented ; with the one h and
we have been spreading cultivation over our own soil and
carrying on the commerce of the universe ; whilst with the
other we have fought successfully against the Tyrant of
the Continent and all his millions of subjects. Our empire
of the sea we have confirmed ; we drove the French out of
Egypt ; Portugal has been rescued ; the emancipation of
Spain is, I trust, at no great distance : every possession
belonging to the enemy in both the Indies has been sub-
dued ; and shall we throw away all these advantages,
arising from abundant circulation—for on that they depend ?
Shall we dismiss a fleet that has ruled the ocean ? Shall
we disband an army, the terror of its opponents ? Shall

we destroy those resources, which, if properly applied, may yet humble Napoleon to the dust? And shall we submit ourselves to a ferocious and to a conquered enemy, merely *to please a band of speculative politicians, the Midases of modern times, who wish to convert everything they touch into gold;* who seem to care but little what experiments they try with the prosperity of the country, provided they can gain a petty triumph by effecting a reduction in the price of their favourite metal, or by diminishing by a few groats or stivers the rate of our exchange; who, contrary to the evidence brought before them, and in opposition to the knowledge and to the conviction of so large a proportion of their fellow-subjects, ventured to report to this House some months ago that our currency was depreciated, and still persist in maintaining so groundless an assertion? But how does it appear that our currency is depreciated? Is it not received as value in all pecuniary transactions? Will it not procure every necessary, every comfort, and every luxury of life? With a sufficient quantity of notes of the Bank of England, cannot the holder of them purchase the most magnificent mansion-house that can be erected, with all its furniture and decorations? Or will they not be received in exchange for the finest, the largest, and the best conditioned estate that the kingdom boasts of? And yet our currency is depreciated!"—*Sir John Sinclair's Memoirs,* vol. ii., p. 269.

But Sir John Sinclair found himself opposed to a majority backed by popular feeling, and he offers the following explanation of the causes which operated to bring about such a change of opinion; for it was only nine years before that Mr. Horner and his followers were defeated by a majority of 144; the numbers being, Ayes 45; Noes 189; whilst in 1819 the House of Commons supported Sir Robert Peel by overwhelming majorities.

Mr.
Horner's
tactics.

"Mr. Horner, the principal advocate for a change, induced Mr. Perceval to allow him to nominate a committee consisting of his own friends, *able and ingenious, but speculative men;* who commenced their inquiries under a firm and immovable conviction that no country could flourish with a paper currency not convertible into coin, and they published a report recommending the resumption of cash payments. The immediate effect was to spread a general alarm throughout the kingdom. Bank of England Stock fell from 276 to 229½; banks began everywhere to lessen their issues; mercantile credit was shaken, and the *Gazette* crowded with insolvencies. These speculative politicians continued their assaults; they were a skilful, numerous, powerful, and above all a united party. Mr. Pitt was no more: Lord Liverpool and Mr. Huskisson were favourable; Mr. Peel unexpectedly became a convert, commencing his career of always conceding to his opponents. Whigs and Tories and Radicals were for the first time united—'when they do agree their unanimity is wonderful.' Last of all, 'under a delirium,' the periodical and daily press inculcated opinions unfavourable to the paper system. Reviews, magazines, and journals began more and more to influence the public mind; and being conducted by theorists and literary men, unacquainted with affairs, they encouraged the popular delusion."—*Sir John Sinclair's Memoirs*, vol. ii., p. 299.

What greatly tended to strengthen the hands of the bullionists was the wording of the bank-note. "The note," they urged, ran, "I promise to pay"—to pay what? why, gold. And is this promise to be broken when the promise is on record "that two years after peace is proclaimed cash payments shall be restored"?

The bank-note a promise to pay gold.

It was argued in vain that the one-pound note was estimated in what it would buy, and not in the quantity of gold which it could command; that it had carried on the home trade successfully; that it had always been received and paid as quittance for twenty shillings of debts and taxes; that the contraction of the currency would alter the present relations of debtor and creditor; that all fixed charges, settlements, and fixed payments would be aggravated to the gain of the creditor and the loss and ruin of the debtor; that the national debt would be converted from a paper obligation, incurred as it was under the paper system, into an obligation to find six thousand tons in gold, or in default of that, to pay in annual interest one hundred tons of gold; that the promise must not be taken to the letter, but was merely an engagement that the note should have a purchasing power to secure to the holder so much of the necessaries and luxuries of life. The parliament in both Houses, and the nation, looked upon all this as special pleading. "It is not so nominated in the bond." The people enthusiastically bowed their necks to the yoke, and entered immediately on such a career of misery and social disruption as had not Prices fall. App. E. been seen "since the Conquest." Prices fell. Corn which had sold at eighty shillings per quarter fell to forty. All other commodities fell in nearly the same proportion. In the year 1812 the average price of wheat was actually one hundred and twenty-two shillings and eightpence per quarter. This price could not have been given had not the nation possessed an abundant circulating medium to give the price. Here, then, was a revolution in price, a revolution more nearly affecting all classes than could any political revolution or even foreign invasion. Sir Robert Walpole had said, eighty years before, that if ever the national debt of this country amounted to one hundred millions, the country would be bankrupt. At the close of the war we had a debt exceeding eight hundred millions—we had expended more than a hundred millions in a single year; we had contracted this debt principally in paper, with a high scale of prices; and our statesmen thought it a primary duty to take steps to compel the people to pay this debt in gold and with low prices. "Never was there a national act of such infatuated ignorance," continues Rector Twells in one of his clear and convincing pamphlets. "The bank reduced its issues; the circulation, which was at its highest in 1813 and 1814, was reduced nearly one-half in 1816 and 1817. In 1815 the average price of wheat fell to sixty-three shillings and eightpence per quarter. The distress was extreme. The great Corn Law of 1815, protecting wheat up to eighty shillings a quarter, was passed. But it failed in securing anything like that price; for how can you by law force men to give more money than they have to give? 'Our Corn Law,' said the late Lord Western to Mr. Attwood, 'was to have secured us eighty shillings a quarter, but it does not.' 'How can it?' was the reply; 'you have passed another law to take away the shillings.' Here lies the gist of the currency question; but the country gentlemen of those days, like the country gentlemen of the present day, whom the late John Stuart Mill irreverently called the 'Stupid Party,' could not understand it. 'It was declared as intricate in its nature, and too abstract for their taste.'"

From 1815 to 1842 there were two systems fighting against each other—Peel's Bills, restricting the supply of money, and making things cheap; and corn laws, passed in the expectation that they would secure a high price, that is, a remunerative price, for corn. The Bill of 1815 was to give eighty shillings a quarter; the average during the eight years it was in operation was sixty-nine shillings and one penny three-farthings. This attempt to secure a high price of corn, when the action of the law was to force cheapness and low prices on manufactured articles, caused an enthusiastic movement against the corn laws, a movement organized by the great Anti Corn Law League, creating an excited state of public feeling only equalled by the Reform agitation of 1832. It was a struggle to make corn, like everything else, cheap. But

[margin notes:] Corn Law to raise prices. Peel's Bill to lower prices.

Lord J. Russell. App. E.

The Anti Corn Law League.

low prices are not remunerative prices. In a highly taxed country, prices, in justice to the producer, ought to rise. He ought to be able to add taxation to price. If twenty shillings represent the price at which the producer can sell an article, and he has taxes to pay amounting in effect to five shillings more, he must sell the article for twenty-five shillings, or he fails to secure the just reward of his labour.

Sir Robert Peel false to his principle.

The vital principle, then, is, to preserve the convertibility of the bank-note; which means, that no note shall be issued unless there be in the coffers of the bank sovereigns to honour it when presented. Good or bad, here is a principle; but how carried out? Sir Robert Peel stumbled at the threshold. He issued £14,000,000 of paper beyond his basis. A grand principle, truly; to maintain which hundreds of thousands, under the influence of periodical panics, have been hurled down from the station in life which long years of patient industry had procured for them, and plunged into misery and distress. For this the poor by millions have been reduced to the bread and water of affliction. The plain fact is, that the vast commercial and industrial transactions of this country cannot, by any ingenious contrivance, be carried on securely for any length of time with a circulation based upon or

Not gold enough in the world.

even nominally convertible into gold. There is not gold enough in the world. Especially is this the case when Germany, Holland, and the United States are following our example and resorting to specie payments. Every expedient is resorted to. The London bankers' clearing house liquidates £1,500,000,000 a year by a comparatively small amount of bank-notes. But all will not do. With a gold standard, all the energies of the country are circumscribed and overpowered.

It may be worth while here to show what a panic is, and what its effects. No one has described them more vividly than Professor Bonamy Price, of Oxford, who, however, remains a strenuous bullionist, in spite of the dire operation of his theory in producing these panics. That this theory is the one in favour with the mercantile body is evidenced by the fact that the Professor, on coming down to lecture in Liverpool, was entertained at a public breakfast by the Chamber of Commerce, when he was complimented on the ability with which he defended the principle of convertibility:—

"I propose to inquire into the nature, the causes, and, if any there be, the means of prevention of commercial crises in England. A graver or a more important inquiry can scarcely arise in the commercial sphere. The symptoms and the effects of these fearful occurrences are, unhappily, but too familiar. It makes men shudder to recollect the agonies which convulse trade at these dreadful seasons—the crash of falling houses; the paralysis and distrust which arrest commerce; the danger hanging over the heads of eminent banks and distinguished firms; the difficulty, or even impossibility, of discount; the sleepless fear of being crushed by the fury of a tempest too violent to be controlled by the wisest or the most experienced. Nor is it merely the memory of the past which gives interest to a question which might seem to belong solely to history. Who among

Bonamy Price on panic.

merchants does not quail at times under a dim consciousness of a mysterious law of periodical recurrence which broods over these trading pestilences? Who is not haunted by a misgiving that the past may repeat itself in the future; that the anxieties and calamities which have marked bygone years revolve in recurring cycles, and may even now be approaching laden with distress and ruin?"—*Lecture delivered to the Liverpool Chamber of Commerce, in October* 1870.

Cheap money, dear commodities, and *vice versâ.*

Panic is the inevitable concomitant of gold, for, being a scarce metal (and its scarcity is its chief recommendation), it cannot keep pace with the immense powers of production evolved by machinery. Every year more and more commodities are produced to be measured against gold, which, though it increases every year, yet becomes relatively scarcer and dearer. It is, in fact, the race between the hare and the tortoise; but coined gold, having a fixed denomination, cannot be said to rise or fall. It is by the rising or falling in price of the commodities estimated in it that dearness and cheapness are expressed; in other words, dear commodities indicate money to be plentiful, cheap commodities indicate money to be scarce. This is well illustrated by Dr. Johnson on his visit to the Isle of Skye,* when told that twenty eggs might be bought for one penny. "Sir," said the Doctor, "I do not gather from this that eggs are plentiful in your island, but that pence are few." It is evident, then, that the free trader's dogma, that cheapness is the synonym of plenty,

Dr. Johnson on cheapness.

* *Tour to the Hebrides,* 1785.

requires modification. To put an extreme case. Reduce the quantity of sovereigns one half, and to what would the price of everything fall? The converse was proved to be true by the influx of Australian gold doubling prices. Indeed, price is all that, in common life, men attend to, and any disquisitions on value, so much indulged in by political economists, are beside the mark. If any one is in doubt whether labour is the actual producer of the wealth, let him consider what would be the situation of this or any other civilized nation, if the labourers should cease their toil for the brief term of five years, letting the earth for that period bring forth only her spontaneous productions. Let man neither sow nor reap, let manufacturing cease, commerce be suspended, and what would be the condition of our country at the end of five years? Would not a large proportion of the people have sunk into their graves from starvation; and would not many who were living be almost naked like the barbarians? If the earth should open her chasms and spew out pure and malleable gold and silver, as plentiful as the rocks in the mountains, it would afford no relief. But if she should cast out wheat, corn and vegetables, beef, pork, mutton, poultry, besides garments, houses, furniture, and so forth, the people would be supplied with the means of subsistence. In such a case we might do without the labour of man. But if we had all the gold and silver money and all the paper obligations that have been made from the creation of the world to the present day, they would not be the least substitute for the produc-

Gold without labour, valueless.

tions of labour ; and yet our laws make these legal instruments in the hands of the few to trample in the dust the
rights of the labourer, on whom we depend for every morsel
of food that we eat, for the clothing we wear, the houses we
live in, and in fact for every comfort and luxury of life.

That paper money is to be the money of the future is
evident from the various steps through which nations
advance in their progress in the paths of civilization.

Bishop
Berkeley.

Bishop Berkeley asks, in the motto on the title page,
"whether, in the rude original of society, the first step
was not the exchange of commodities; the next, the substitution of metals by weight, as the common medium of circulation; after this, the making use of coin; lastly, a
further refinement, by the use of paper with proper marks
and signatures ; and whether this, as it is the last, so it be
not the greatest improvement ?"

CHAPTER IV.

"Gold money, scarce money—scarce money, dear money—dear money is usury."

SIR JOHN SINCLAIR, in his Memoirs, declares that "it was a great discovery when a metallic medium was substituted for barter; it was also a great discovery when paper convertible into coin was substituted for gold and silver; but a third discovery was reserved for our own times, namely, that with an inconvertible paper currency, agriculture, commerce, and manufactures might advance in a career of unexampled prosperity."

What will chiefly aid in forcing a paper money on the attention of the civilized world, will be the break-up of the Funding system; the first symptoms of which have already been shown by the bankruptcy of the Turkish and Egyptian Governments, who find themselves totally unable to meet the interest on their debts; whilst the tottering credit of some other States indicates that this liability to pay in gold debts owing chiefly to foreigners, is coming to be questioned. These public debts, if looked into closely, are only a machinery for mortgaging the labour of generations unborn, adding to the constantly increasing power of the

Break-up of Funding system.

monied or creditor interest. This is not only evident in
England, but on the Continent, and in recent times in the
United States, and should be a matter for serious reflection
to all not totally absorbed in the personal battle of life.
To use a vulgar phrase, the English nation—leaving out
the millionaires, the monied men, and the wealthy—is " on
the penny." Everything is calculated in money. Even the
tithes, which a few years back were taken in kind, are now
commuted into a money payment. The first great item in
this stupendous system of indebtedness is that of national
obligation, our own debt mounting up to £800,000,000. If
to this we add the debt of the United States, £600,000,000,
and those of the Continental States, which *Haydn's Book
of Dates* gives at £2,500,000,000, and the Indian debt,
£40,000,000, it will be seen that the nations of the civilized
world are labouring under a burthen which must in time be
simply unbearable. That this borrowing system is breaking
up becomes apparent when we find that, like a chain cable
with a failing link, it has broken down in its weakest part.
Egypt and Turkey have failed to pay their creditors a
dividend, and as the United States have resolved to carry
on their internal trade on the gold basis, it is simply impossible that they will have any to spare for the foreign
fundholder. Their repudiation is only a question of time,
for, however willing to keep faith, they cannot perform
impossibilities. At this very time Germany has resolved on
specie, that is, gold payments, as also has Holland; and
there is not the quantity of this metal on the face of the

Indebted-
ness,
national
and pri-
vate.
App. F.

earth to meet all these requirements. Nor are *we* quite secure. "We have taken a bond of fate, and nothing can touch us," our newspapers and Chancellors of the Exchequer tell us. But this cloud in the East may burst. We may find ourselves involved in a war sooner or later, and then our expenditure, if the Crimean campaign is to be taken as a guide, will add £50,000,000 a year to our debt. The public attention will be directed to the means of raising this additional taxation; but for this where must we look ? Obviously to the land. But the House of Commons will strenuously resist a land tax, and then it is to be feared there will be a letting out of waters—that then will be the beginning of troubles.

So much for national debts. But let us look at private indebtedness. Is there a young man beginning a trade or opening a shop who is not in debt to some monied man ? Nearly all the trade of the country is carried on by credit. Then comes the vast system of mortgage. It is not too much to say that one-third of the land and houses in this country are mortgaged, and as the mortgager is at certainties and the mortgagee at uncertainties, Lord Bacon assures us that "at the end of the game the money will be found in the money bag." The municipal corporations are in debt £40,000,000. This implies heavier rates. What the rate-payers in London have to pay for their "vast improvements," as Cobbett called them, is something appalling, and a crisis is at hand nearer than is generally supposed. The local taxation in this town (Liverpool), is assuming formidable dimensions. Gas-works, water-works, insurance companies, and limited liability companies, are so many associations whose claims add to the indebtedness of the community, and whose dividend generally runs up to 10 per cent. As to limited liability companies, they are a new machinery for any man who can save his hundred sovereigns to join the annuitant class, and in time to get out of trade or productive industry. But as some of them are non-paying, the evil is somewhat mitigated. In fact, trade and the productive energies of the country are so loaded with rent, interest of money, and taxation, that they are beginning to succumb; and this accounts for the wretched state of the iron, coal, cotton, and other trades. Universal depression is the rule in this year of our Lord 1876, and we have indicated the cause.

Gold-digging a waste of of labour.

Gold money must be scarce money, scarce money must be dear money, and dear money is only another name for usury. The first step in this complication of error is the diversion of labour from the useful occupations of tilling the ground, constructing railways, laying out good roads, building more roomy and commodious cottages, to that of digging, crushing, riddling, and washing quartz reefs in Australia. It is there that we see this absurd waste of that most sacred of all things, labour, withdrawing more than 50,000 men from adding to their own and the community's stores of food, clothing, and lodging,—from contributing to the comforts and even elegancies of life, and devoting themselves to a degrading and precarious occupation, reduced to a state of primitive barbarism, and experiencing all the privations of savage life.

The demoralising effects of this search are beginning to make themselves felt in these colonies. A complete lottery of a few great prizes and of many blanks fosters a spirit of gambling. The despair of the losers, and their regrets over a life of wasted labour, drive them to forget their troubles in intoxication; while the sudden acquisition of wealth by the more fortunate adventurers finds them totally unprepared by education and early association to spend it with judgment or taste. The extraordinary spectacle is thus presented to the world of a " navvy aristocracy."

A ' navvy' aristocracy.

This search for the precious metal is stimulated by the price—£4 an ounce, as fixed by law; that is, the Bank of England must buy all bullion offered to it. It might be a matter of curious speculation what the price would be if the nations of the earth were wise enough to demonetise it.

Price of gold if demonetised.

And yet, much as California and Australia have added to our stock, production, stimulated by this supply of its great want, money, still asks for more. It is still relatively scarce, and usury, the scourge of nations and the crying sin of. the age, is still ravaging industry and inflicting incalculable evils on mankind.

CHAPTER V.

"Not the accumulation of wealth, but its distribution, to be considered."
—JONATHAN DUNCAN.

A SHORT review of what usury effected in ancient times is thus described by Sismondi, who attributes the decline of the Roman Empire to this insidious and cursed concomitant to metallic money :—

"As nations advance in what is popularly called civilization, there has ever been a tendency to concentrate riches in the hands of a few; and as the idle classes increase, they who produce most consume least. It is this injustice, through its prime agent, usury, that led to the downfall of all the great nations of antiquity ; for if labour builds up a State, labour alone can sustain a State; degrade labour, and you sap the foundations on which the super-structure rests. So it happened in ancient Rome in what are deemed its palmiest days of civilization.

Usury the principal cause of the downfall of the Roman Empire.

"During the entire ages of Trajan and the Antonines, a succession of virtuous and philosophic emperors followed each other ; the world was at peace ; the laws were wise and well administered; riches seemed to increase ; each succeeding generation raised palaces more splendid, monuments and public edifices more sumptuous than the preceding; the senatorial families found their revenues increase; the treasury levied greater imposts. But it is not on the mass of wealth, it is on its distribution, that the prosperity of States depends; increasing opulence continued to meet the eye, but man became more miserable; the rural population, formerly active, robust, and energetic, were succeeded by a foreign race; while the inhabitants of towns sank in vice and idleness, and perished in the midst of riches they themselves had created."

Such is a picture of Rome under the Emperors; but usury was a crying evil even in the simpler times of the Republic, and though struggles between the patricians and the plebeians seemed ostensibly to turn on land, yet the money-lender was at work, and frequent allusions are made to his influence on the condition of the people.

Lord Macaulay brings forward, as one of the grievances of the plebeians, their being ground down to the dust by the barbarous and unjust legislation touching pecuniary contracts. "The ruling class was a monied class; and it made and administered the laws with a view solely to its own interest. Thus the relation between the lender and the borrower was mixed up with the relation between sovereign and subject. The great men held a great portion of the community [he might be talking of England] in dependence by means of advances at enormous interest. The law of debt, framed by the creditors, and for the protection of creditors, was the most horrible known among

Macaulay on usury in Rome.

men. The liberty, and even the life, of the insolvent were at the mercy of the patrician money-lenders."

Not only had whole provinces become the property of an individual, but usury existed in so frightful a form that even the virtuous Brutus, when Pro-Consul of Sicily, received 60 per cent. for the loan of money (this is vouched for by his friend Cicero); whence we may form some idea of the extortions of those who were less scrupulous. What must have been the income of Agrippa, who, at his own expense, built the Pantheon, and supplied Rome with one hundred fountains, all ornamented with marble columns and statues ? The colleague of Cicero was proprietor of the whole island of Cephalonia, on which he built an entire city. In the time of Nero it was ascertained that six Romans were in possession of half of Africa, and it would be easy to mention the names of many others enjoying colossal fortunes. Now, Pliny expressly says that these immense agglomerations of wealth, which he also declares ruined Italy and the provinces, were due to the concentration of estates, which he terms "latifundia," and to usury. The words are " Fœnus hoc fecit, et nummus percussus."

Here we see the evils of concentrated wealth; and as this wealth accumulated, men decayed,—not because wealth accumulated, but because it was inequitably distributed.

The legislation of Sir Robert Peel and Mr. Jones Loyd (made Lord Overstone by Lord John Russell), tends to realize in these days the same injustice and consequent ruin which occasioned the downfall of Rome.

Usury was equally rampant in Greece, if the representa- tions of Aristophanes and the denunciations of the orators and moralists may be believed. It was owing to the infatuated belief, so prevalent in half-civilized nations, that gold and silver should be money, that Athens maintained her supremacy over the other States. It was the mines of silver at Laurium which, by making her the source of money, and *that* supplied on her own terms to her neighbours, made this insignificant district the supreme power. This is entirely overlooked by Grote, Mitford, and Gillies, for thus far all history has been in the hands of writers imbued with the prejudices of their times. Even Gibbon holds forth frequently on great stores of gold, silver, and precious stones, as indicative of abounding wealth. In fact, history will have to be written over again, with the aid of lights thrown on it by a sound financial theory.

If we pursue our inquiry into the Middle Ages, we shall find that this besetting and yet little noticed sin has attracted the attention of the Church more than the State.

The ancient Fathers speak of it in no measured terms; but they had no idea of a true representative or certificate of labour. However much mistaken in matters of doctrine and discipline, on this they were correct; and though they cannot be acquitted of pride, and undue authority, there were manifest honesty, sincerity, and good intentions. Merchandise, as they saw it practised, was a series of frauds;

indeed, it is not much better in these days. But the principle of equivalents, as clearly stated by Mr. Ruskin, would enable merchants and traders to pass goods from producer to consumer with honour and credit to themselves, and without violating the sacred laws of justice in the operation.

Amongst these Fathers may be named St. Thomas, Ambrose, Tertullian, St. Gregory of Nyssa. Mr. Bentham sets their invectives down to superstition, but it may be doubted if the charge of superstition might not be retorted.

The Councils of Terracon, also, anno 516; of Nice, anno 325; of Lyons, anno 1273; of the Lateran, anno 1179; of Pope Martin, anno 572,—all denounce this curse, and forbid all ranks, especially the clergy, to indulge in these practices. One example must suffice :—

" Nothing exceeds this modern system of usury ; indeed, these usurers traffic in other people's misfortunes; taking gain through their adversity; under the appearance of compassion they dig for the distressed a pit of misery; under the appearance of giving to the indigent, extending the hand to relieve him who harbours from the storm, by alluring him only to be shipwrecked upon the shoals and shallows of an unforeseen whirlpool. A dreadful disease, my dearest brethren, affects the Church ; a disease calling loudly for a speedy remedy. Commanded not to lock up our money, even the product of our honest industry, and to hold our house ever open to receive the poor, we collect riches through their wants ; flattering ourselves that we have discovered an excusable system of avarice and rapine. Your riches were given you to relieve the poor, but not to plunge them into misery. Why have you abandoned your God in order to follow horrid riches? Are you not aware that this practice is forbidden in the Old Testament also? . . . Should you consult also the dispositions of temporal laws on the matter, you will find that usury has been always considered a mark of the most barefaced impudence."—*St. Chrysostom, in his Homily on St. Matthew.*

The Church of England denounces usury, classing it with the most odious of vices. For in the Canon 109 the following occurs: "If any offend their brethren either by adultery, whoredom, incest, or drunkenness, or by swearing, ribaldry, or USURY, or any other uncleanness, the churchwarden shall present them, that they shall be punished, and not admitted to the Holy Communion." This is little attended to by men in holy orders, and no class is more ready to invest in foreign loans, tempted by high and usurious interest, than the curates and vicars and rectors of the Church of England. Their names frequently occur in lists of bank shareholders, and of investors in insurance companies. Who ever heard a sermon holding forth usury as a sin? Are they not too ready to pay court to the richer members of their congregations, without any reference to the equivocal modes in which those riches are acquired? Nor can dissenting ministers be acquitted of passing over the crying sin of the age in silence, though well aware that "the chief places in the synagogue" are chiefly held by men indulging in these iniquitous transactions.

Canons of the Church of England.

4

The Jews
.isurers.
App. G.
The greatest usurers in the Middle Ages were the Jews, whose extortionate claims were the principal cause of the popular hatred which too often found vent in massacres and persecutions ; and these not discouraged by kings, emperors, and princes, embarrassed by the demands of their unscru-
Carlyle on
parch-
ments.
pulous creditors. Mr. Carlyle in his graphic way describes the relations which subsisted between King and Jew: "Parchments! yes, parchments are venerable, but they should at all times represent, as near as they can, the writings of the Rhadamanthine tables, otherwise they are not so venerable. Benedict the Jew in vain pleaded parchments—his usuries were too many. The King said, 'Go to: for all thy parchments, thou shalt pay just debt; or observe this tooth forceps.'"

And Sir Walter Scott, in his Ivanhoe, brings out their usurious practices in his picturesque way. Advancing to later times, we have the Greshams, the Fuggers, the Guys, the Hopkins (immortalized by Pope), and the Medici. The name of a street in London tells us whence banking and scrivening were introduced. Lorenzo de Medici, the Mag-
Lorenzo de
Medici.
nificent, derived his enormous riches from loaning and banking, for we are told by Mr. Roscoe that the immense revenues of this family were derived from the banks which they had established in all the trading cities of Éurope, and which were conducted by agents in whom they placed great confidence. At a time when the rate of interest frequently depended on the necessities of the borrower, and was in most cases very exorbitant, an inconceivable profit must have

been derived from these establishments. Sovereigns might be found among their debtors, and in the list occurs the name of our Edward the Fourth.

Historians have been too much occupied with the intrigues of courts, with campaigns and the fate of battles and the vicissitudes of war, to watch closely and take note of the insidious encroachments of this social canker. The tyranny of the government, the contests of party and faction, the privileges of the nobles, are sufficiently dwelt upon, but the exactions of the monied class are passed over. In the histories of France, the oppressions of the noblesse, and of the farmers of the taxes, are duly noted, but the exactions of money-lenders, scriveners, and mortgagers of land and house are passed over. Erckman Chatrian, in his *Histoire d'un Paysan*, tells us how farmer and peasant are ground to the earth by their inevitable and law-protected demands:

"On parle quelque fois de maladies que vous rongent le cœur, que vous dissechent le sang:—mais le vrai maladie des pauvres, le voilà! Ce sont les usuriers, ces gens qui se donnent encore l'air de vous aider, et qui vivent sur vous jusqu á ce que vous soyez sous terre. Alors ils tâchent de se retrapper sur la veuve et les enfans."

John Law, with his Mississippi scheme, is held up as a warning to future generations of the dangers of paper money; but a candid consideration of his proposal will show that his prophetic visions of the future New Orleans, and of the boundless fertility of that immense valley of which it was to be the port, were founded on a sure basis.

John Law, M.P.

Like all great men, he was before his time. The Duke of
Orleans, and the profligate courtiers, made this daring but,
as a century has shown, not absurd speculation, into a mere
excuse for stock-jobbing.   Bishop Berkeley asks in his
Querist, "Whether the ruinous effects of the Mississippi,
South Sea, and such schemes, were not owing to an abuse
of paper money, or credit, in making it a means of idleness
and gambling, instead of a motive and help to industry?"
As to the South Sea Bubble, Australia and New Zealand
have shown that reality will sometimes outstrip the wildest
speculations.   Even El Dorado had some foundation in fact.
These were all of them too early anticipations of what
maritime discovery afterwards revealed.

The same causes produce the same effects.   Other
countries of Europe could tell their tale of robbery under
cover of law, though perhaps Poland, under the iron grasp
of the dominant race, the Jews, may be emphatically cited,
since under this race, so devoted to the pursuit of gain, that
country has never been able to emerge from a state of semi-
barbarism.

Galway.   In the county Galway, in the region of Connemara, lies
an immense tract of country, consisting of unreclaimed bog.
This was the estate of the late John Martin.   The tourist
enters on this desolate district by Martin's Gate, and travels
through this wilderness by means of Bianconi cars for
twenty miles, when he arrives at Ballynahinch.   Mr.
Martin died hopelessly in debt, chiefly through the cessation of the demand for kelp; and his sister sailed to America

in a state of great destitution. His estates are now in the hands of a London Insurance Company, who are more at home in financing than in improving lands. We have here square miles of bog, and a population who, under the stimulus of constant employment and good wages, would find the labour. As bog is only excess of vegetable matter, the correctives, clay-marl, and sand, with arterial drainage, would fertilise this barren waste; but all is stopped for want of money. Now for a proposal which will make the hair of every politico-economical professor stand on end. MAKE MONEY! Issue a paper based on the prospective labour brought into play by this constituent of wealth.

The large estates in the north of Ireland are, on the contrary, carefully cultivated. They are under the London City Companies, who, by liberal treatment of their tenants, City Companies in diffuse comfort and happiness around. As has been pithily north of Ireland. expressed, the City Companies, being easy landlords, "manure the land with rent." The difference between the north and west of Ireland is obvious to the most careless observer.

As a contrast to this account of Connemara, the following extract from the *Glasgow Herald* shows a wise expenditure, on the part of the Duke of Sutherland, of capital, as the *Times* would call it, but which is really an expenditure of money. Here would be a legitimate basis for an issue. The waste land is there, and the labour. All that is wanted is—money. The Duke does not apparently agree with the political economists in their dogma, "Don't cultivate inferior soils":—

" A remarkable experiment, the result of which will have
an important bearing upon a great question of the day, has
been going on in the far north during the last four years.
The Duke of Sutherland, who makes up for his silence in
the arena of public life by a good deal of practical wisdom
exhibited in other directions, is carrying to a successful
issue an undertaking which cannot fail to bring honour to
his own name and advantage to his country. He has proposed to bring under cultivation by steam power 2,000 acres
of wild and useless moorland, lay it out in farms of considerable size, erect farm buildings, and, on the success of
the experiment, continue the operation wherever waste and
barren land exists on his property. It is satisfactory to
know that the Duke's efforts have succeeded almost beyond
expectation. The land reclaimed has now yielded a second
crop. We hear of an average crop of oats, a fair crop of
barley, more than an average growth of turnips, an excellent crop of hay, and good fields of potatoes. These results
have not been reached without a very considerable outlay
both of money and labour."

In the *Times* of the 31st October appears an interesting
letter from Mr. Mitchell Henry, M.P. for Galway, who,
stimulated by the example of the Duke of Sutherland, has
taken a large tract of bog-land in hand, and is bringing it
into cultivation.

Here we see Manchester money at work. The capital
will be the labour embodied in fencing, draining, liming, etc.

This contrast between Scotland and Ireland makes it

plain that on no people would a sufficient supply of money confer more benefit. There we see land and labour divorced, and this owing to scarcity of money. The ring is wanted that should marry these two essentials to the production of Ireland. wealth. England, by her manufactures, is constantly draining Ireland. The rents of the landlords, mostly absentees, are drawn in gold.

The particular feature which distinguishes Ireland is the extent of the bogs. Advances of Exchequer notes might be made, did the law permit it, on the landlords engaging to devote themselves to their cultivation. Of course precautions would have to be taken that they were not diverted to claret, hunters, or trips to Paris.

If next we turn to India, we find those immense popula- India. tions ground to the earth. There the Schroff (the native money-lender), the Armenian, and the Parsee reign supreme. The rates of interest prevailing are so shamefully exorbitant that no labour—the ultimate source from which all interest must be derived—can possibly meet its demands. The prevailing rates are from 10 to 20 per cent. Such immense profits arising from such flagrant usury is too much even for British virtue, for one of our best Governors felt himself bound to bear the following testimony :—

"Sir Charles Metcalfe, it will be seen, was witness to the same nefarious doings as those of Hastings, Clive, Impey, and Benfield, denounced so eloquently by Edmund Burke. It is evident that, under the rupee system, these cruel exactions are still as barefaced and extortionate as ever,

He found not merely the normal state of affairs in the Nizam's court and country—corruption, extortion, the most atrocious mismanagement and consequent anarchy, for all of which, of course, he was prepared beforehand; he found what was far worse—British subjects, and those not solely persons unconnected with the public service, engaged in the illicit and unrighteous trade of the Hyderabad money-lenders, exacting from a miserable people interest at the rate of 25 per cent., and backed to a lamentable extent by the highest authority in India."—*Edinburgh Review*, July, 1855.

Proposal to coin the silver.

And by a happy coincidence, a means of extrication from this lamentable state of things presents itself in the extraordinary influx of silver from California. And yet under the influence of inveterate prejudice, this accession fills the authorities of Calcutta with perplexity and alarm, for they see no way to extricate themselves from the consequences. Yet here is presented to them a relief from the great oppression which afflicts the Hindoo population,—their dependence on the Schroffs, the native money-dealers. Coin this superabundance of silver into rupees. Confer on each disc of silver the money denomination, making it a legal tender for debts and taxes. Silver is at once preserved from depreciation. The poor Hindoo would at once be furnished with the means of paying his debts, and he would be released from the fangs of these merciless exactors. India is indeed a notable example of the cruelty and insanity of rulers exacting taxation and not giving the taxpayer the wherewithal to pay it in.

The late James Wilson, who was promoted from the editorship of the *Economist* to be the financial minister of India, was so impressed by what he saw, that, according to the late Jonathan Duncan, who had it from good authority, he was seriously resolved to endeavour to introduce taxation paper money. It would have been a stupendous task to have carried this reform to a successful issue in the face of the opposition of the officials, alluded to in Sir Charles Metcalfe's Memoirs, backed by the power of the native money-dealers and the Parsees.

The *Times*, which cannot at all times control the out- spoken opinions of its correspondents, inserted in an unguarded moment the following exposure of the miserable *laissez faire* notions prevailing:—

" We have left the zemindar and the usurer to reduce this people to positive slavery. The zemindar and his *amlah* (underlings) take 10-16ths of the ryots' crops—imagine that!—and the usurer steps in and takes the other 6-16ths, and the people live upon the advances of the latter from one year's end to the other. Growing the most magnificent harvests of wheat, rice, opium, indigo, they themselves starve on the coarsest millets, and are as poor and miserable as can be conceived. In these circumstances I have urged privately, but with all the force I could command, the only counsels that can save us from a very awful calamity, viz., the empowering the ryot to take the crops now in the field and the cold-weather crops, suspending all claims upon him for rent, advances, revenue, etc., for twelve months. If the customary misappropriation of these crops between zemindar and usurer takes place this year, nothing will save the people, I am persuaded, from perishing by millions."

The Colonies.

If from India we turn to the Colonies, we find the same cause still at work—no provision made for supplying them with this the life-blood of trade. They are indebted for what they have to the sums brought by emigrants and to what balances of exchange may be in their favour in trading with foreigners; and if the British sovereign is not forthcoming, the Spanish dollar is welcome. Australia must be excepted. More fortunate than her sister Colonies, she found the coveted treasure at her feet, and with the aid of her Mint supplied herself with what has conferred upon her a prosperity in remarkable contrast to the others.

CHAPTER VI.

HOW CAN PAPER MONEY INCREASE THE WEALTH OF A NATION ? " ANSWERED.

WE must now come to the most striking instance of the opposite results of the two systems, as furnished by the United States of America. We can trace their workings in this now powerful nation from its origin as British plantations to the present year (1877), when the controversy between "Hard Money and Soft Money" has become a leading hustings question. But as no one has put this in a clearer light than the late lamented Rector Twells, brother to the Member for London, the following extract from his pamphlet is now given :—

Opposite results of the two systems.

" To many persons it appears impossible that bits of paper inscribed with certain characters can promote the prosperity of a nation, or increase its wealth. But if the prosperity of a country be promoted by the facility afforded to its inhabitants to exchange what each possesses for what he requires, a medium of exchange inexpensive in itself and capable of expansion with the wants of the country, and with its increasing population, must be highly beneficial.

The question proposed shall not, however, at present be answered by explaining the true theory of money, but by an appeal to *facts*. Land and labour being admitted to be the primary sources of a nation's wealth, let *facts* show how Paper Money assists land and labour to create wealth.

Prosperity of the American colonies. "Look, first, at the great fact of the prosperity and wealth of the United States of America. As a testimony to their growing prosperity, let us take a short extract from a speech of Edmund Burke, on American Taxation, delivered in the House of Commons so far back as the 14th of April, 1774. Alluding to the Americans, he says :—

" '*Nothing in the history of mankind is like their progress.* For my part, I never cast my eye on their commerce, and their cultivated and commodious life, but they seem to me rather nations grown to perfection through a long series of fortunate events, and a train of successful industry accumulating wealth in many centuries, than the colonies of yesterday—than a set of miserable outcasts, a few years ago, not so much sent as thrown on the bleak and barren shore of a desolate wilderness, three thousand miles from all civilized intercourse.'

" Such is the recorded opinion of this distinguished statesman.

" And how was this miracle effected ? David Hume the historian shall answer that question. Here is an extract from his correspondence with the Abbé Morellet :—

" ' In our colony of Pennsylvania, *the land itself*, which is the chief commodity, *is coined, and passes into circulation.* A planter, immediately he purchases any land, can go to a public office and receive notes to the amount of half the value of his land, which notes he employs in all payments, and they circulate through the colony by convention. To prevent the public being overwhelmed by this representative money, there are two means employed : first, the notes issued to any one planter must not exceed a certain sum, whatever may be the value of the land ; secondly, every planter is obliged to pay back into the public office, every year, one-tenth of his notes. The whole is of course annihilated in ten years, after which it is again allowed him to take out new notes, to half the value of his land.'

"This was the monetary system under which the American colonists prospered to such an extent that Burke said of them, 'Nothing in the history of the world is like their progress.' It was a wise and beneficial system, and its effects were most conducive to the happiness of the people. Take the case of a family industrious and enterprising, driven by persecution or misfortune to seek a refuge in the wilds of the new world. With their scanty means they purchased a tract of land. Many years of hard labour, privation, and anxiety would have been necessary to bring that family into a state of decent competency, had they been required to purchase gold and silver by labour and by the produce of labour, before they could effect other improvements of their property. *But half the value of* Paper Money on land.

*his land was advanced to the head of the family in notes,
which circulated as money.* With these notes he could hire
labour, and purchase implements of husbandry, and cattle;
and thus where without these notes one acre could be
cleared, cultivated, and stocked in a year, ten would, by the
assistance of the paper money advanced, be reclaimed from
the forest and rendered productive. Thus hope entered the
dwelling of the poor emigrant. Ten years found him,
with the whole of his debt to Government discharged, the
proprietor of a happy home. And the kind hand of a
paternal Government was stretched out still, to advance to
him again one-half of the increased value of his land, and
thus enable him to clear more of the forest, and to settle
his children in new homes. Such was the system by which
' a set of miserable outcasts' were converted, in a short
space of time, into happy, contented, and prosperous
colonists.

" A prosperous people are generally well satisfied with
the form of government under which they live.

Metallic
money sub-
stituted.

" When, in 1776, Dr. Franklin was examined before a
Committee of the whole House of Commons, he was asked,
' What was the temper of America towards Great Britain
before 1773 ?' He answered, ' *The best in the world.*
They submitted willingly to the government of the Crown,
and paid in all their courts obedience to Acts of Parliament.
Numerous as the people are in the several old provinces,
they cost you nothing in forts, citadels, garrisons, or armies,
to keep them in subjection. They were governed by this

country at the expense only of a little pen, ink, and paper. They were led by a thread. *They had not only a regard but an affection for Great Britain*, for its laws, its customs, its manners, and even a fondness for its fashions that greatly increased its commerce. *Natives of Britain were always treated with particular regard; and to be an Old England man was, of itself, a character of some respect, and gave a kind of rank among us.'*

"In an evil hour, the British Government took away from America its 'representative money;' commanded that no more paper 'bills of credit should be issued, that they should cease to be a legal tender,' and collected the taxes in hard silver. This was in 1773. Now mark the consequences. This contraction of the circulating medium paralyzed all the industrial energies of the people. Ruin seized upon these once flourishing Colonies; the most severe distress was brought home to every interest and every family; discontent was urged on to desperation ; till at last ' human nature,' as Dr. Johnson phrases it, 'arose and asserted its rights.' In 1775, the American Congress first met in Philadelphia. In 1776, America became an Independent State.* *American colonies rebel.*

"Again, Sir A. Alison, the able and indefatigable historian, bears this testimony to the power and superiority of Paper Money. 'When sixteen hundred thousand men were engaged in active warfare, on the two sides, in Germany and Spain alone, where nothing could be purchased but by *Sir A. Alison. Paper issued by the allied sovereigns.*

* This, the real cause of the disaffection of the American Colonies, is passed over by most historians.

specie, it is not surprising that guineas went where they were so much needed, and bore so high a price. In truth, such was the demand for the precious metals, owing to that cause, that at length all the currency of the world, attracted to Germany, as a common centre, could not supply it; and by a decree on September 30th, 1813, from Peterswaldau in Germany, the allied sovereigns issued paper notes, guaranteed by Russia, Prussia, and England, which soon passed as cash from Kamtchatkha to the Rhine, and produced the currency which brought the war to its successful issue. There was an instance of the manner in which a paper circulation, based on proper security, supports credit, and supplies the want of specie at the decisive moment. Whereas, according to the present system, the paper would of necessity have been contracted, when the specie became scarce— credit would have been ruined at the critical period, *and the vast armaments of the allies would have been dissolved for want of funds for their support.'—England in* 1815 *and* 1845, p. 76, 77.

"And in a recent edition of the history of Europe, he gives this additional evidence of the important advantages which EXPERIENCE HAS DEMONSTRATED to result from a paper currency. 'To the suspension of cash payments by the Act of 1797, and its power, in consequence, vested in the Bank of England, of expanding its paper circulation in proportion to the abstraction of the metallic currency and the wants of the country, and resting the national industry on a basis not liable to be taken away either by the muta-

Suspension of cash payments.

tions of commerce or the necessities of the war, *the salva-tion of the empire is beyond all question to be ascribed.* It *is remarkable that this admirable system, which may be truly called the* MOVING POWER OF THE NATION *during the war, became towards its close the object of the most deter-mined hostility on the part of both the great capitalists and chief writers on political economy in the country.* Here, however, as everywhere else, EXPERIENCE, THE GREAT TEST OF TRUTH, HAS DETERMINED THE QUESTION. The adoption of the opposite system of contracting the paper in propor-tion to the abstraction of the metallic currency, by the Acts of 1819 and 1844 (followed as it was necessarily by the monetary crises of 1825, 1839, and 1847), *has demonstrated beyond a doubt that it was in the system of an expansive currency that Great Britain, during the war, found the sole means of its salvation.'—Alison's "History of Europe,"* vol. xx., p. 79-80.

Hostility of capitalists.

" And, moreover, the *fact* that, from 1797 to 1815, com-merce, manufactures, and agriculture advanced (in spite of all the evils of war) *with a rapidity greater than they had previously done in centuries*, proves still further the power of*Paper Money to increase the wealth of a nation.*

" The monetary policy of England since the termination of the war in 1815 is a warning to all nations. The greater part of the national debt had been contracted in what was called a ' depreciated ' paper currency, with a high scale of prices. Our legislators determined to make the people pay this debt in gold, with a reduced scale of prices. In

Gold money the cause of panic.

5

this manner from 30 to 50 per cent. was added to the burden which the people of England had to endure. And not only so, but, by the contraction of the circulating medium, the productive industry of the country was checked and enterprise impeded. The burden of the people was made heavier by the monetary system, which simultaneously diminished their strength. The distress, privation, confusion, and ruin which in 1816, 1819, 1825, 1837, 1839, 1847, 1857, and 1866 this fatal mistake entailed on this nation are ascertained and undeniable.

Gold, the money of barbarism. Paper money, the money of civilization.

"The monetary legislation of 1819 was a step backwards. Peel had not the power of destroying the system of Paper Money. Had he been able to do so, and had he done it, the nation would have retrograded as speedily as it had advanced. But Peel's Bill *crippled* the monetary system which Mr. Pitt had introduced. Peel went as far as he dared in restoring an exclusively metallic money—*the money of the early ages of barbarism.* Nor shall we ever permanently prosper as a nation till we return to a representative Paper Money—*the money of civilization and progress*—money which is capable of expanding with expanding wealth and increasing population—money based upon the great truth that a nation's wealth consists not only in the precious metals which are drawn out of the mine, but that there is wealth lying hid in the nerves and sinews of the labourer, the enterprise of the merchant, the skill of the artizan, the discoveries of science; which, therefore, gives to every wealth-producing power of man, to land,

and to labour—no less than to gold and silver—its *repre-sentative*, as well as its *actual* value—money provided by the Government for the use of the people, in which debts can be discharged and taxes paid — money neither of intrinsic value, nor convertible into any fixed amount of any commodity whatever, and which is therefore secured from undue inflation when gold is brought into the country, and undue contraction when gold is withdrawn from the country;— ENGLISH MONEY FOR THE ENGLISH PEOPLE; and, obviously, American money for the American people."
—*Rector Twells's Pamphlet.*

The same results have manifested themselves in America which we experienced in (England) 1819. Nor is it America or England alone that feel themselves compelled to resort to this expedient in a time of war. Other nations invariably betake themselves to this efficacious alternative; which, however, will prove its wonderful power in a time of peace as well. *[Paper money in time of war.]*

The swamp has to be drained,—cultivation has to creep up the sides of the hills,—roads have to be levelled,— railways require cuttings and embankments,—water has to be brought to the towns from distant lakes,—harbours of refuge established,—bogs to be reclaimed,—arterial drainage to be engineered,—sewerage to be carried to the land instead of poisoning the rivers,—towns and cities to be rebuilt, and the whole country to be made into a garden. *[In time of peace.]*

Why should not these peaceful contests with nature be carried on with energy and sustained efforts ? There is

Paper money would employ criminals and paupers.

the labour, and there is the raw material. Bring these into combination, and you have wealth, or, to use the Saxon root, wellth—everything conducing to well-being. There are thousands of men able and willing to work. Nay, if need be, take your criminals and paupers, who would soon assume new characters if they had organized work before them on the plan sketched by Mr. Carlyle.

What stops the way ?

WANT OF MONEY.

There is the simple remedy—*make money* under State supervision and under parliamentary control. Affix to your State-document the signature of the Chancellor of the Exchequer, engaging to recognise such issue as legal tender, like Mr. Pitt's one-pound note, and the thing is done.

America arrested in her progress.

Both ancient and modern history tell the same tale. America has already been referred to as a great country, which was advancing in a career of unexampled prosperity, and suddenly arrested in her course, as testified by one of her citizens (*vide* page 77), who has drawn a picture of her state—a picture which must have wrung his heart— of bankruptcy, distress, and fiscal demoralization. That the tale is true, the ebbing tide of immigration tells us. The model republic is no more a land of promise. There, as with us, wealth in abundance avails not where the distribution is unjust and imperfect.

Distribution of wealth.

Political economy has hitherto confined its inquiry to the production of wealth, but the distribution of wealth is the more important, and the instrument of distribution must be taken into account, and an attempt must be made to rescue it from illogical and confused speculation.

. " What can be more heartless," writes Jonathan Duncan, " than the following extract from Adam Smith's ' Wealth of Nations,' in which the leading idea seems to be that the wealth produced by labour must be appropriated by the money lord, the landlord, the fund-holder, and the annuitant or the leisure class, and only enough left to the labourer to maintain him and find him in sustenance enough to give him strength to continue his labour? This is in direct opposition to the principle that the labourer is worthy of his hire, and that the reward of his industry should be secured to him with as few deductions as possible—that he shall receive the total amount of that reward—that, labour being the source of all wealth, to the labourer's share, if possible, all the wealth should come; and by labour is meant all well-directed industry in the highest branches of intellect and skill, as well as in mere manual labour; and that the claims of landlord and money lord should be severely looked into.

Adam Smith's heartless doctrine.

" But let us hear what Adam Smith says :—

" ' The produce of labour constitutes the natural recompense or wages of labour.

" ' In that original state of things which precedes both the appropriation of land and the accumulation of stock, the whole produce of labour belongs to the labourer. He has neither landlord nor master to share with him.

" ' Had this state continued, the wages of labour would

have augmented with all those improvements in its productive powers to which the division of labour gives occasion; all things would gradually become cheaper. They would have been produced by a smaller quantity of labour; and as the commodities produced by equal quantities of labour would naturally in this state of things be exchanged for one another, they would have been purchased likewise with the produce of a smaller quantity.

"'But this original state of things, in which the labourer enjoyed the whole produce of his own labour, could not last beyond the first introduction of the appropriation of land and the accumulation of stock.* It was at an end, therefore, long before the most considerable improvements were made in the productive powers of labour, and it *would be to no purpose to trace further* what might have been its effects upon the recompense or wages of labour.'

Jonathan
Duncan's
comments. "The passage underlined is the condemnation of Adam Smith's work. He commences by truly describing the just relations which once existed between the producer and products; and what is just ought to be permanent. If the appropriation of land and the accumulation of stock necessarily wrought injustice, and robbed the labourer of his fair recompense, they ought to have been condemned; nevertheless, had these two processes not come into existence, what is termed civilization would not have been known. Adam Smith, as a teacher, ought to have solved

* Adam Smith in this day would have added machinery; but when he wrote, its wonderful powers were not developed.

the industrial problem, instead of declaring that 'it would be to no purpose to trace it to its ultimate consequences.' To solve this and other industrial problems was the end, aim, and purpose of his work.

" In another sentence Adam Smith writes thus :—

"'What are the common wages of labour, depends every-where upon the contract usually made between those parties whose interests are by no means the same. The workman desires to get as much and the master to give as little as possible.' Here he indicates a perpetual antagonism of classes, without making the slightest effort to harmonise interests which are really identical. *Adam Smith on wages.*

"'No society,' continues he, 'can surely be flourishing and happy, of which the far greater part of the members are poor and miserable. It is but equity, besides, that they who feed, clothe, and lodge the whole body of the people' should have such a share of the produce of their own labour as to be themselves *tolerably* well fed, lodged, and clothed.'

" The equity of the case," continues Mr. Duncan, commenting on this word *tolerably*, " is indisputable, especially as in the natural state of things, according to Adam Smith, the whole produce of labour belongs to the labourer, who then has neither landlord nor master to share with him. And what a mighty boon does Adam Smith confer upon those who feed, lodge, and clothe the people, when he simply insists, in his narrow view of equity, that they who perform this great work should themselves be *tolerably* well fed, clothed, and lodged!" *On the word ol-erab*

Mr. Duncan quotes another passage, which he truly describes as absolutely revolting :—

" 'The wear and tear of a slave, it has been said, is at the expense of his master; but that of a free servant is at his own expense. The wear and tear of the latter is, however, in reality, as much at the expense of his master as that of the former. The wages paid to journeymen and servants of every kind must be such as may enable them, one with another, to continue the race of journeymen and servants, according as the increasing, diminishing, or stationary demand of the society may happen to require. But though the wear and tear of a free servant be equally at the expense of his master, it generally costs him much less than that of a slave. It appears, accordingly, from the experience of all ages and nations, I believe, that the work done by freemen comes cheaper in the end than that performed by slaves.'

" Sentiments so heartless merit unqualified reprobation ; but Adam Smith does not accompany them with a single word of censure. He accepts them as expressing an inevitable condition of society. Journeymen and servants are permitted, in this system of political (political certainly, but not social) economy to multiply a race of operatives sufficient to minister to the wants and luxuries of the rich— that is, those living on rent and interest of money; but that limit they must not overstep. In point of industrial reward, the free labourer is worse off than the slave ; for though he produces more, he receives less, so that his nominal liberty is a mere delusion.

"'It deserves to be remarked,' says Adam Smith, 'that it is in the progressive state, while society is advancing to the further acquisition, rather than when it has acquired its *full complement, of riches*, that the condition of the labouring poor, of the great body of the people, seems to be the happiest and most comfortable. It is hard in the stationary, and miserable in the declining state. The progressive state is in reality the cheerful and the hearty state to all the different orders of society. The stationary is dull; the declining melancholy.' Here it may be asked, What is to be understood by the full complement of riches? Surely the term is vague, if not meaningless. This 'fulness' is a point to which society is ever tending, but never reaches. If every man, woman, and child had a constant command over all that they desired to possess—if all were well fed, well clothed, well lodged, and well educated—and if the labouring classes were relieved from the excessive toil they are compelled to endure, and had leisure to cultivate their minds and invigorate their bodies—it might be said, and yet only in a hypothetical sense, that a 'full complement of riches' had been realized; but the phrase would still be loose and imperfect, for were such an advance in social progression attained, it would only be a new point from which to start in a new race.

"David Hume had a deeper insight, for he points out the true condition on which alone society is enabled to make ceaseless progress from epoch to epoch.

"'In every kingdom into which money begins to flow in

greater abundance than formerly, everything begins to take a new face: labour and industry gain new life; the merchant becomes more enterprising, the manufacturer more skilful and diligent, and even the farmer follows his plough with greater alacrity and attention. The good policy of the magistrate consists only in keeping it, if possible, still increasing; because by that means he keeps alive a spirit of industry in the nation, and increases the stock of labour in which consists all honour and riches.'

"The comments made on Adam Smith's chapter on wages have been introduced for the purpose of pointing out the wide difference that exists between the science of political

Political economy versus social economy.

economy and the science of society. The former simply calculates the product and forgets the producer; the latter proclaims that the labourer is worthy of his hire, lifts him from the degradation of being a mere hewer of wood and drawer of water, recognises the dignity of manhood in every class, and insists on the equitable distribution of wealth. The school of Adam Smith, solely intent on material things, and forgetting persons, has vainly endeavoured to establish a social equilibrium ; and though it has taught many useful truths in reference to the division of labour and the production of wealth, it has done nothing to elevate the standard of humanity. It does not profess to take any heed of morals, or of the feelings and affections. Its philosophy dwells on insentient matter, not on sentient beings. Certainly this utilitarian school has a right to adopt its own course, and if it did not venture beyond the sphere of accountants and statisticians, no fault could be found with its teachings; but when it succeeds in infusing its false and heartless precepts into practical legislation, it becomes dangerous to society. This school forgets that wealth, rightly understood, is not an essence but an attribute, and that its nature changes with the persons and the things to which it is attributed. To accumulate riches and place them beyond the reach of producers, is simply to realize the fable of Tantalus."—*Jonathan Duncan on the Bank Charter.*

CHAPTER VII.

"A nation deprived of a due supply of money, suffers like the prisoners in the black hole of Calcutta, and like them it will offer all it is worth to any one who will supply it with that without which it suffers commercial syncope. Now is the time for the 'hard calculator' and usurer."

TO the American mind, less enslaved to conventional ideas, and more ready to accept bold innovations, we must look for fearless investigation and inquiry less trammelled by stereotyped opinion.

The Western States enthusiastic and organized.
One hopeful sign is, that the great Western States, rapidly developing in population and wealth, are pronouncing more and more emphatically every day for Paper Money, and it is to the Eastern States chiefly that the "Hard Money" men look for support in their efforts to make the nation pay gold interest on a Greenback debt. The sufferings they are undergoing—the exact counterpart of ours in 1820—are opening their eyes, and the controversy is assuming a more determined and inveterate aspect every day. In a previous page Mr. Tierney, Sir James Graham, and Mr. Attwood have been brought forward to bear testimony, and protests as energetic are being pronounced there. They, too, see bankruptcy decimating their manu-

facturers, distress harassing their middle class, employment denied the working-men, and—an additional grievance
—immigration from Europe stopped. A few only of these
protests are now given.

Mr. Samuel Seaville read before the Industrial Congress
which met at Rochester, April 11th, 1874, the following
statement of the present condition of this once happy fede-
ration of prosperous republics. It must indeed be galling
to the feelings of an American citizen thus to bring before
the eyes of the once despised Europe this humiliating
picture :—

Mr. S. Sea-
ville on
American
demoraliza-
tion.

"In this land we behold a strong young nation drunken
with the new wine of freedom and of external prosperity.
Dazzled by sudden growth in wealth, and by wondrous developments in science, it forgets the lessons taught by the
fathers, and turns its back upon the ways of rectitude in
domestic, social, commercial, and political life. Everywhere
is disintegration. Shams and eternal verities totter for the
time. Cries of alarm are heard on all sides. Pious usurers
rejoice that, at last, it is easy and pleasant 'to do right;'
and that their lusty cry for 'Specie Basis' enables them to
righteously 'devour widows' houses, and grind the faces of
the poor.' The inventions of genius, grasped by the shrewd
and forceful, turn and devour the people as the demon
created by Frankenstein destroyed its creator. Steam
(which should have lifted half their burdens from the
heavy-laden working classes, doubled their incomes, and reduced their hours of labour one-half) more and more dis-

places human creatures,* and is used to double the tasks
of those still allowed to be its co-workers. It gives us a
thousand million man-power; yet the 'protected industries'
of New England give 'hands' less than $400 a year, in
the average, and shriek of coming doom when 'eight hours
labour' is mentioned; while every few years a 'great'
manufacturer dies 'worth' from five to fifteen millions.
Our young men, crazed by the success of men of small
capacity all about them, shun honest labour, and press
toward city sinecures. Our women, robbed by steam and
machinery of their vaunted 'home industries,'—spinning,
weaving, knitting, making clothes, soap, cheese, brooms,
baskets, etc., are following those industries into the cities,
to their own destruction. Even their clothes are now
largely imported—ready-made by German paupers. Europe
pours upon us her paupers and knavish traders, and Asia
sends the overflow of her debased millions to drag down
our children to their own level. Absenteeism prevails.
American capitalists rob our producers and poorer consumers, to spend the plunder upon European middlemen.
Our boasted modern amenities are all steeped in fraud.
Life insurance, for instance, is, in the average, a monstrous
swindle. In one recent year, lapse and surrender annulled
93 per cent. of the terminated policies."

Dorman B. Eaton says: "It is part of the scheme of
those practising frauds, that the laws be made so compli-
cated that none but a trained villain can understand them."

The Americans have taken up this question with all their

accustomed energy and ability. They are well versed in
the various English writers who have investigated and
studied the question.

The following is a powerful appeal to the people against
the annual drain of gold to pay the foreign fund-holders
interest on their bonds, and the consequences resulting:—

"SIR,—Foreign debt, carrying gold interest, is what is *The foreign gold debt.*
crushing the hearts and the hopes and undermining the
morals of the labouring people of our country. It is that
indebtedness which is filling our almshouses with people
skilled in many industries and eager to toil for their living.
It is that foreign debt, that annual gold indebtedness for
interest on the principal, that is stripping the thrifty and
industrious labourer of his earnings hoarded through years
in savings banks; that is compelling him to see his humble
but mortgaged home pass to the capitalist at a nominal
price, because he has not been permitted to earn the little
stipend that would enable him to pay his monthly dues to
the building association, or his semi-annual instalment to
the capitalist. It is that foreign debt which is causing a
vast tide of emigration to flow from our shores, and repelling
hundreds of thousands of immigrants who hoped and expected to find shelter, freedom, and prosperity under our
republican institutions."

Whilst another speaker quotes Sir Thomas More: "So
help me God, I can perceive nothing but a certain con-
spiracy of rich men, procuring their own commodities
under the title of commonwealth. They invent and devise

all means and craft, first how to keep safely, without fear of losing, what they have unjustly gathered together; and next how to hire and choose the work and labour for as little money as may be." *

Even the Eastern States confess to the sad state to which the country is reduced, and to the intense animosities engendered between the "hard" and "soft" money advocates.

The *Philadelphia Ledger*, by the following extract, makes it plain that the Eastern States are gradually becoming alive to the fact that the Greenback question is at the bottom of it all, and such protests find their way into the newspapers in spite of the vigilant control of the capitalists :—

The
Phil-
adelphia
Ledger on
the dis-
tress.

"The times are pretty hard, the signs of which are unmistakable. The 'Wants' columns of *The Ledger* are quite full, but these are not all. There are long lists of horses and carriages for sale—'property of gentlemen going abroad'—which tell tales of sudden vicissitudes and collapse. 'Board at summer prices,' is the delicate way in which landladies announce compulsory reductions. Sales at auction, by marshals, by sheriffs, by mortgagees, by pawnbrokers, of every possible variety of article of luxury, stare at one from the newspaper page. And the announcement of 'reduced prices for clothing,' for 'fuel,' 'flour,' and other necessities tells the same story. Painful facts to contemplate, but they have to be faced; and the moral they teach of the need of strict economy ought not to be over-

* For Extracts from "The Money Question," by W. A. Berkey, Michigan, see App. H.

looked. We have not yet done paying the penalty for false prosperity which followed the war, and will continue through the Paper Money period. All kinds of business are very much prostrated. The capitalists are accepting lower rates of interest, and the holders of stock investments are generally becoming satisfied with 6 per cent. interest, and even 5 per cent., if the payment of that smaller rate is fully assured. Hundreds and thousands are out of employment, and all, rich and poor, are gradually coming down to humbler pretensions. The 'penalty' will continue through the Paper Money period. How long will that continue? For my part, I fear it will be long; and such is the mischievous reaction in these cases, the check to prosperity, on which my contemporary enlarges, will most seriously retard the return to specie payments after which his soul obviously lusts. But for the benefit of my readers, who may not be familiar with American finance, and the intense animosity with which its hostile theories are discussed, I will tell them that a very demonstrative party in the State denounces the high finance, of whose programme this return to a metallic currency is one of the principal pillars. They insist that the salvation of the country is only to be secured by subverting the old-fashioned policy—which there is such a struggle to restore—and that radically new banking practices and new currency laws will be necessary to avert national bankruptcy. They say it is coming on their country rapidly. I regard this growing controversy without further comment than this: That such extreme diver- Angry controversy.

6

gence of opinions, and such heated contentions, are at least very unlikely to contribute to that common and harmonious effort which is doubtless required to restore prosperity to trade and commerce. This angry controversy is, doubtless, both an effect and a cause. It is an effect of the discontent which restricted trade engenders, and it will prove a powerful obstacle to the restoration of prosperity."

The angry controversy will become more and more embittered, for the monopolists and high financiers will not give up their control over the country till the American people compel them.

The French deprived of all their gold.

To the Americans we are indebted for publishing and making known the late great financial operation of the French nation, who have given us two extreme examples: the one, of the deplorable effects of over-issue in the assignats; and the other, of the wonderful and beneficial results of a paper issue under control and wise management in their late contest with Germany. Our writers on finance are lost in perplexity when they see how France quickly recovered herself, though all her gold was abstracted, and how distress and bankruptcy and diminished trade were concomitant with the Germans' acquisition of this same gold. M. Victor Bonnet, an eminent French political economist, says of the late financial experience of that nation:—

M. Victor Bonnet on the issue of 1,800 millions.

"What has taken place in France since the war in relation to the paper circulation, what is still taking place to-day, is a very curious phenomenon. It apparently reverses the economical and financial principles which the best authorities on the subject have hitherto laboured to establish. They have cautioned us against issuing too much Paper Money, having the quality of legal tender; holding that the volume of such paper should be very carefully limited, lest confidence in it should become impaired, and depreciation follow. Now it so happened that, almost at a single step, in the midst of our disasters, we issued more than 1,800 million francs of new notes, and that this legal tender paper has kept itself at par, the only time when it fell below par being upon the payment of the first instalment of the indemnity to Germany."

It would indeed be long before we should have this plain statement of these wonderful results from the *Times*, from the professors of political economy, or the reviewers in this country; but the Americans are being roused to an intense interest in the inquiry, " for, from the depths of their present miserable state, they look back to the time when Greenbacks—in spite of the excessive drain of their civil war—not only fed and clothed and equipped armies on their destructive mission, but vivified their prostrate industries, and developed production to a hitherto unprecedented * extent and activity, until peace resumed her sway, when it was found to be fully as beneficial an agent for construction as for destruction, for wealth as for waste, and, consequently, for happiness, comfort, and content, as it had hitherto been in the battle-field for the purposes of devastation and havoc.

The Americans roused to inquiry.

Paper money in peace as in war.

* Not unprecedented. See Mr. Burke's eloquent description (p. 60) of the happy, contented, and flourishing condition of these same United States when, as colonies, they enjoyed a paper based on land.

"The exigencies of war, in addition to their great purpose, the striking the shackles from the limbs of the black race, had for the first time in history produced money 'by the people, of the people, and for the people.' 'Every working man was busy. Taxes were heavy, but work was plenty. Our national indebtedness was being paid off. Homesteads were cleared from mortgages, and it did seem as if our approaching centennial would show the world a republic fairly completed in fact, as well as in law,—free and independent in finance, as in religion and politics. The 'Unproductives,' however, are still animated by their ancient spirit, and being the chief makers of the laws for the protection of labour and ingenuity, the increase of products, and the change and transfer of property, they shape all their devices so cunningly that they, the 'Unproducers,' continue to grow richer than the producers."—*J. G. Drew, of Elizabeth, N. J.*

These "Unproductives," headed and influenced by the Wall Street speculators, have reduced the country to a debasing dependence on the London gold-market, as thus depicted:—

"The commanding issue of to-day is a struggle of supremacy between producers and combined monopolies; between the creators of wealth and those who do not create, but who, by large combinations and ingenious devices, absorb more and more of the wealth produced, especially that central monopoly, the grand focus of all monopolies, the money power.

"This power is not merely the bankocracy of the United

States, which, influential as it may be in commerce, industry, and the halls of legislation, is nevertheless but one subordinate constituent of that universal power, that 'international imperialism' which has its chief centre in London, its co-ordinates in every nation, its branches in every principal city in Christendom, its correspondents wherever property is bought and sold, which controls the money of the world through the control of gold, and so determines the rates of interest and the prices of money, of products, and of labour; which excites industry into full activity by copious loans, and, at pleasure, collapses every interest by calling in gold, or attacking credit; which fattens upon public debt and private misfortune, for it more than doubles the volume of debt and the cost of railways by discounting government and railway bonds, so that in many cases less than fifty per cent. of loans goes to legitimate use; buys private property at panic prices and real estate at foreclosure sales; which dominates cabinets, dictates diplomacy, shapes legislation, nominates executives, inserts its plank in party platforms, interferes in elections, forms coalitions, instructs finance committees, procures boards-of-trade resolutions and memorials, inspires presidential vetoes, manufactures public opinion through the press and public meetings, lobbies in every legislature on the globe, levies double and three-fold tributes upon the labourer, producer, manufacturer, carrier, consumer in all lands, and, withal, is irresponsible.

"A single illustrative fact may be suggestive: August Belmont, American representative of the Rothschilds, was

for many years Chairman of the National Executive Committee of the Democratic Party.

"Recent developments have alarmed this omnipresent
power, and its varied resources will be freely used to maintain its prerogatives and perpetuate its control of all interests.
On the other side are the useful classes of every name, and
their first necessity is ORGANIZATION.

*   *   *   *   *   *

Pauperism.   "Then we display to the astonished world a country
which for its size, its agriculture, its manufacturing and
commercial advantages, surpasses any other nation recorded in history, in proof of which, did we not export
last year nearly £400,000,000 of bread stuffs and cotton?
Yet our republic presented to the gaze of mankind last
fall and winter (1875) the greatest incongruity of any
other nation that ever existed, when hundreds of thousands
of native-born American mechanics were reduced to the
first step towards pauperism—when they approached soup
houses as mendicants, with blushing countenances and
aching hearts, while corn by the ten thousand bushels was
consumed in the west for fuel; and, to add to our shame,
thousands of foreign artizans left this boasted country during
the September panic, and returned to their respective
countries to obtain employment, whereby to preserve their
true manhood[and dignity.

*   *   *   *   *   *

Green-
backs.   "This is what we see: that while our producers have
begged almost on their bended knees for the privilege—

the right to labour, and to be paid for the same in national Interest-bearing Bonds. certificates of indebtedness, called Greenbacks, without interest, our infatuated Government has insisted on having its work done by subjects of European monarchies, and to pay for the same in interest-bearing bonds; and that our mechanics are leaving our shores to find that employment which we have banished across the ocean.

" If this has not been practically levying a tariff upon our home productions, or offering a bonus on foreign importations, we have forgotten what little cyphering we ever knew.

" We have, as a nation, substituted idleness for industry, poverty for affluence, beggary for thrift, restlessness for contentment, emigration for immigration, foreign subserviency for domestic independence.

" Under the mighty influence of a national money we America follows the example of England. evoked the national resources. We followed the example of England in the Napoleonic wars, who with it, and by it, won Waterloo and conquered Napoleon. France, in her late contest with Germany, did act so promptly that it never fell below $1\frac{1}{2}$ per cent. discount. And in our own recent struggle, though too blindly adhering to a superstitious reverence and worship for the spiritualistic and mysterious power of gold, we found ourselves abandoned by it before the heavy work of war fairly began, when the Greenback took up, and with ease, the work abandoned by its weak and cowardly competitors." *

This successful attempt of the " Unproductives " to thrust

* " Political Economy for the People."—*J. G. Drew.*

this "money of barbarism" on this once prosperous nation had a precedent in 1832.

General Jackson *versus* General Harrison.

General Jackson, in 1832, copying Peel, endeavoured to introduce a metallic currency in America; ruin followed; the bank of Pennsylvania stopped. America had in a few years, as Burke said, made the progress of centuries; that was with Paper Money. The attempt to introduce metallic money perilled their commercial prosperity, and they abandoned it. " If," said General Harrison, the President in 1840, " any single scheme could produce the effect of arresting at once that mutation of condition by which thousands of our fellow-creatures by their industry and enterprise are raised to the possession of wealth, that is one. If there be one measure better calculated than another to produce that state of things so much deprecated by all true republicans, by which the rich are daily adding to their hoards, and the poor sinking into penury, it is an exclusive metallic currency. Or if there is a process by which the character of the country for generosity and nobleness of feeling may be destroyed by the great increase and necessary toleration of usury, it is an exclusive metallic currency."

The excuse for these copious extracts must be the fact, as stated by Professor Bonamy Price (p. 5), " that the defence of an inconvertible paper may be said to have disappeared from English literature."

In fact, the Americans, in their true "go-ahead" character, seem to dive deeper into the slough of error, and get out of it quicker than we do on this side of the Atlantic.

The development of the monied men into a landed aristocracy is rapidly taking place. The Railways alone have allotted to them blocks of land on the lines larger than the area of England. By means of land companies they are becoming possessed of immense tracts of land, which they sell off in lots as settlers increase in numbers, "so that," says Mr. Drew, "if we are not fools we will note the next step taken by England, and be very sure that, as in the past we have adopted her theories in finance, and thus so far repeated her history, if we continue to follow this same leadership, we shall have to wallow through the same terrible experience which has reduced the landowners in England in number from 160,000 to 30,000 in 1861, though the aggregate population in that time, thirty-nine years, must have been more than doubled."

The monied men becoming a landed aristocracy.

To show how lack of money paralyzes industry, impedes the circulation and exchange of productions, increases bankruptcy, and inflicts incalculable suffering on the debtor and working interest, the following table is given by the same authority.

"The mercantile failures in the Northern States, from 1862 to 1870, inclusive, which we copy from *Hunt's Magazine and Year-Book* for 1870, were:—

Years.	Currency per head.	Number of failures.	Aggregate liabilities.
1862	—	1,652	$23,049,000
1863	—	495	7,899,000
1864	$40	520	8,579,000
1865	30	530	17,625,000
1866	24	632	47,333,000

Currency per head.

Years.	Currency per head.	Number of failures.	Aggregate liabilities.
1867	$19	2,386	$86,218,000
1868	17	2,197	57,275,000
1869	16	2,411	65,246,000
1870	14	3,160	79,697,000

"We supplement the foregoing table with the following (for the whole nation) of commercial failures for 1870, 1871, **Failures.** 1872, and 1873 :—

Years.	Number of failures.	Aggregate liabilities.
1870	3,551	$88,242,000
1871	2,915	85,252,000
1872	4,069	121,056,000
1873	5,181	228,490,000

"The failures of 1873 are about 25 per cent. in excess of 1872; but the aggregate is nearly double, showing that devastation is spreading among the loftier commercial and financial circles."—*J. G. Drew.*

This tallies with our experience, for the *Times* informs us, that from 1846 to 1857, 90 banks broke, with liabilities amounting to 47 millions.

CHAPTER VIII.

" A sovereign laid out at compound interest at the birth of Christ would amount to a larger mass of gold than the bulk of the earth.''

THE Usury Laws were abolished by Sir Robert Peel at the very time he was making money dear by making the sovereign our only money. This let loose the rapacious harpies who prey on the extravagance of youth and on the necessities of the needy tradesman. Instances are continually cropping up in the newspapers, but the most recent and notorious was the case of Sanderson and an Oxford student. Those wholesome restrictions removed, and we have loan societies devastating the middle classes, whilst the pawnbroker preys on the labourer and artificer. The banks fly at higher game, and their enormous dividends, and this whether trade be good or bad (the London and Westminster, for instance, with its 20 per cent.), point out the cancer which is eating into the body politic.

COMPOUND INTEREST.—To the workings of that baneful offspring of the system we owe those immense masses of wealth which are left by will, and which are duly chronicled in the newspapers. The *Illustrated London News*, at

[margin note: Usury Laws abolished.]

[margin note: Compound interest.]

' stated intervals, gives a list of these, confining itself to those only above a quarter of a million.

These agglomerations are entirely the fruit of compound interest, the operation of which has not attracted the notice of the political economists.

Immense accumulations above quarter of a million. App. I. In the Appendix I. is given a list of a hundred men wh in the last ten years have died worth £60,000,000—no one inserted whose legacies are less than a quarter of a million. There are two put down at £3,000,000 each. Let us pick out one with his £3,000,000. The interest on this colossal fortune at 3 per cent. is £90,000. Let us suppose this leviathan of wealth to spend per annum £40,000; here is a sum of £50,000 with which to go into the investment Millionaires seeking investment. market. Investment! the great trouble of millionaires, filling them with anxiety, and costing sleepless nights:—coal mines, landed estates, consols, foreign loans, railways, gas, water, and insurance shares:—they must be distracted by variety of choice, whilst begging letters for donations to churches and a hundred charities must lay daily siege to the knockers of their mansions. The very finance must require a staff of clerks and collectors not much less than that of many public bodies.

But to return to his annual saving of £50,000. We must bear in mind that it accrues year by year. Let us take our example at his thirtieth year, and let him reach his seventieth, and what immense accumulation do we see. 40 × 50,000, if Cocker may be depended upon, will amount to two millions. The working of the extraordinary engine of usury is something wonderful. Suppose one of those mil- lionaires was able to secure 10 per cent.,—and some of them by sagacity in choice, say fortunate investments in coal-mines, secure more than this,—and we have these immense accretions doubling themselves in seven years. One thousand pounds would stand thus in the forty years on which limitation our calculation is based :—

Our capitalist begins in his 20th year with £1,000.

In his 27th year the £1,000 becomes			2,000
„	34th	„	2,000	„	4,000
„	41st	„	4,000	„	8,000
„	48th	„	8,000	„	16,000
„	55th	„	16,000	„	32,000
„	62nd	„	32,000	„	64,000
„	69th	„	64,000	„	128,000

Impossible, it may be said. Perhaps so; let us cut off one-half, and there remain £64,000, usurious and monstrous progeny of the original £1,000; and yet, as the Usury Laws are abolished, these immense sums are recoverable by law. Can the productive powers of the earth keep pace with such claims? Are sovereigns coined in quantities sufficient to give them the monetary expression?

Surely the end of this is not far off.

All this must end in social revolt and popular discontent. Carlyle gives us an ugly picture in his "French Revolution" of the fate of a Dives—one Foulon. Foulon, a few years before the breaking out of the French Revolution, had told the people who had crowded round his bureau in a time of

distress that "they might go and eat grass:" fatal words! as
may be seen in the sequel.

"Sansculottism drags him from his hiding place: Sansculottism seizes him.   His body is dragged through the streets,
his head goes aloft on a pike—'*the mouth filled with grass*'—
amid sounds of Tophet from a grass-eating people."

If history is experience teaching from example, here is a
lesson.

10 per cent. too much for trade.
Such are the vast accumulations which a rate of interest
calculated at 10 per cent. produces, but 5 per cent. even is
more than legitimate trade can bear.

De Foe on interest.
De Foe, in his "Complete English Tradesman," depicts the
inevitable ruin of a tradesman resorting to borrowed money
even at the moderate rate of 5 per cent., unless he can
avoid two contingencies which unfortunately attach to all
trade,—the giving of credit and the avoidance of losses.
He says:—

"In a word, interest of money is a canker-worm upon the
tradesman's profits: it consumes him unawares.   Not one
tradesman in fifty states to himself the true nature of it; it
eats through his ready money—for it takes nothing for payment but its own kind; it makes no defalcation or abate-
ment for bad debts, or disasters of any kind; whatever
loss the tradesman meets with, the USURER must be paid;
whoever the tradesman compounds with, HE makes no com-
position, unless it is at last of all, and he is forced by the
ruin of the tradesman to compound for both interest and
principal, when perhaps, by the mere interest, he had had

his principal two or three times over; and this brings me to another terrible article upon a tradesman, and that is —extortion. Increased by extortion.

" It is thus fatal to the tradesman to pay but the moderate interest of the money at 5 per cent. which we call lawful interest; what then must it be, when he is encroached upon either by the lender, or, which is as bad, by the procurer or scrivener or banker, under the sly and ruinous articles called procuration, continuation, premium, and the like ? These are when the poor debtor is apparently in need of a loan, and it appears that he is not in a condition to refund the money, and though perhaps he has given good security for the money ; so that they are in no danger of losing it, yet these people never want artifices or pretences to hook in new and frequent considerations by way of addition to the ordinary interest."

No one has put the matter in a stronger light than an old writer whose name has not reached us. He says:— Usury by an old writer.

" Whoever borrows at usury condemns himself to poverty. The borrower is not relieved, he is only embarrassed. The usurer's life is both indolent and insatiable ; he gathers his harvest when he sows his seed. He awakes richer in the morning than he was over night. Desist, O man, from your dangerous cares, from your precarious calculations : seek no offspring from gold and silver, things naturally barren."

The common phrase so prevalent, that such a man has " made money," shows the common idea that a man can in Making money.

some mysterious way aid the mint in its particular function of coining, and that by skill in trade, improvements in manufactures, success in speculation, and even by accumulating money at interest, he increases the money of the country. The slightest reflection should dispel the delusion. Wealth may increase in a country, the houses may become villas, the clothing may be more plentiful, the land may be made to produce more, machinery may aid in various processes of manufactures, docks and harbours be excavated, railways intersect every county,—but all this does not add to the quantity of money. MONEY has been well defined as a conventional instrument adopted by civilized nations to secure the justice and avoid the disadvantages of barter; CAPITAL, as the accumulated labour of preceding generations, constantly added to by the labours of the living generation. Under the gold theory it is the mint only that can make money.

Take the instance of a man clearing a thousand pounds by a speculation. What he gains, another man loses. Peter is robbed to pay Paul, but there is no addition to the money of the country.

CHAPTER IX.

" Usury the scourge of nations and the crying sin of the day."

BUT usury has its defenders, and the most celebrated is Jeremy Bentham, whose "Defence of Usury" is the text-book which is put forward as its most able vindication. It required some courage to stand up for a system which has been condemned in all nations and in all ages, "*quod semper, quod ubique, quod ab omnibus.*"

Bentham's " Defence of Usury."

Let us examine this leading proposition as laid down by Mr. Bentham :—

"What natural fixed price can there be for the use of money more than for any other thing?"—(P. 9, "Defence of Usury.")

Because money is endowed with certain privileges. The coined gold, the sovereign, is legal tender; in it only can you pay debts and taxes. The money denomination withdraws it from the list of commodities, and gives it special functions,—commodities in one scale, money in the other; thus we know that if money is cheap, commodities are dear; if money is dear, commodities are cheap.

" Custom, therefore, is the sole basis on which the legis-

7

lator can build his injunctions, but what basis can be more weak than custom arising from free choice ?" (P. 10.)

Free choice ! The freedom is not very perceptible, when the borrower must have it, if he is to pay a debt or a tax, and the lender can take advantage of his need.

" Antecedently to custom growing from convention, there can be no such thing as usury."

Money is a conventional instrument to obviate barter, and the custom, usury, came into existence when convention superseded barter.

" Nor has blind custom any steadiness. Among the Romans, 12 per cent. ; in England, in Henry VIII.'s time, 10 per cent., afterwards reduced to .5. In Hindostan, where there is no rate limited by law, the lowest customary rate is 10 or 12." (P. 11.)

So it is confessed that where the law does not interfere the rate may rise to 12. Here it may be asked, Is any labour so profitable that it will bear any such imposition ?

" Now of all these widely different rates, which one is there which is intrinsically better than another ? " (P. 12.)

Lowest rate of interest the best. Yes ! The lowest is the best. All interest is a deduction from the reward of labour. As seen in the case of Turkey, high interest is ruin.

" Much has not been done, I think, by legislators as yet in the way of fixing the price of other commodities." (P. 13.)

Money not a commodity. This is the grand error which throws Mr. Bentham wrong. MONEY IS NOT A COMMODITY. Take the sovereign: the act of the mint in coining this disc of gold, with the king's head on one side, and the British arms on the other, withdraws it from the list of commodities, as the pound weight is withdrawn from the list of the articles it weighs. This disc of gold is MONEY, in which all commodities are priced;—it is legal tender, in which alone the debtor can pay his debts. This disc of gold once monetised, no debtor can pay his debt in kind: his creditor may demand payment in the lawful coin of the realm, and can, under the sanction of law, refuse payment in corn, cloth, fuel, or any other commodity the debtor may deal in.

Such a flagrant error as calling coined gold a commodity leavens the whole sixty pages of this "Defence," the style of which is offensively dogmatic.

Chapter IX. puts the case of horses and money on the same footing, but if horses are not legal tender, and money is, the argument goes for nothing. Horses won't pay debts or taxes: to do that, they must be sold,—they must pass through the gold mill.

Mr. Bentham puts the case of horses.

Chapter XVI. defends compound interest without limitation, so that, in Mr. Bentham's eyes, the rate of 30 per cent.—a rate ruling at Constantinople—is as proper and legitimate as a rate of 5 per cent.; and this is his illustration:

Defends compound interest.

"I who have money to lend, and Titius who wants to borrow it of me, would be glad, the one to accept, the other to give an interest somewhat higher than my neighbours. Why is the liberty they exercise, that of dealing at a certain rate of interest, to be made a pretence for depriving me and Titius of ours?"

Well, for Titius let us substitute a money dealer in Turkey. He, under liberty of contract, stipulated for 30 per cent., and as his unfortunate debtor is most likely unable to pay the debt of say £100 the second year, compound interest at 30 per cent. is . . . . £130. In three years the debtor finds the claim against him doubled,—£200 !

Mr. Bentham defends this last invention of Mammon, devised in one of his wickedest moods, by which a sovereign laid out at the birth of Christ would amount to a mass of gold equal to the bulk of the earth. These "hard calculators" are magicians of a high order, to endow a sovereign with power to multiply itself a hundred-fold ! Let us take the instance of such a financier accumulating £1,000 a year, and this for fifty years. This sum, by simple lying by, would be £50,000. Again, suppose the case of the same sum, £1,000, put out at compound interest at 10 per cent. for the same period—50 years, and the £1,000 becomes £120,000 ! But if to this we add year by year a thousand pounds put by at the same rate of interest— and how many monied men heap up many thousands ?—the results become fabulous. But this "multiplying figures" is mere vanity and vexation of spirit, for the sovereigns which make it negotiable are not in existence; there is not the money to represent it, nor is labour—the source of all wealth—able to meet its demands, which yet are recoverable by law. The simple question that disposes of these nefarious exactions—the very progeny of usury—is, "Do corn, wool, cotton; do fuel, furniture, houses, increase in the same ratio ?"

Accumulations of compound interest.

Such are the results of a high rate of interest. One of the great benefits of a low rate is, that the wings of a compound interest are clipped, since it takes twenty-four years for a sum of money to double itself at 3 per cent. Compound interest is the natural result of simple interest, and its injurious working can only be counteracted by keeping the rate low.

The first principles of society are trampled upon by this prostration of industry at the feet of avarice and fraud. Sir Robert Peel made money scarce, and then abolished the Usury Laws. And we see, every day, one man preying upon another, and all mutual advantage lost sight of, in the certain loss, if not utter ruin, of one of the parties. To what purpose is the property of the subject protected by the laws from the robber and the thief, who can only take what is possessed at present, if the arm of the insatiable hoarder, of the despised yet power-wielding miser, may stretch out with impunity to the future, to rob to the furthest verge of life, and to prey upon unborn generations ?

If thievery is penal, why not usury?

" In society, no transaction is more frequent than loan ; none more needful, none that lies so open to avarice, none where extortion can inflict so deep an injury.

" But in loans, when do the parties meet on equal terms ? The one lends from his abundance, the other borrows from his necessity. The very nature of the contract proves that the one holds an advantage over the other.

" It may be asked, must we of necessity borrow from this particular monied man ? Oftentimes we must. Every man

must borrow where he is known; for example, he may be
known but to one banker: his condition may be such that
he cannot or dare not borrow from another.

"But granting him liberty, will the change of creditor
better his condition? Will it make his need the less?
Shift as often as he will, the original difference remains.
Lender's
advantage
over
borrower. The one lends from his abundance, the other borrows from
his necessity. In short, they grapple, not on equal ground—
the borrower is undermost.

"Again, extortion or usury has characters of its own which
mark it as more dangerous than other frauds. In other
frauds detection for the most part affords security for the
future; but in usury the borrower knows that he is
defrauded without daring to complain—extortion begets
Accumula-
tive power
of interest. extortion, 'and the fraud,' as Dumolin justly says, 'is
continued, aggravated, and multiplied, through a succession
of years, ending commonly with the ruin of its victim.'

"Closely connected with this is another reason why usury
is of such danger to society, proceeding from the nature of
interest, which, by its incessant increase and prodigious
multiplication, differs from all those things, whether of
nature or of art, by which interest is paid. They have
their times of rest; not so interest,—its progress is incessant. And it is for this reason that compound interest is
forbidden in most states."—*Hannay's "Defence of the Usury
Laws."*

Lord
Bacon. Another reason is the one already quoted, assigned by
Lord Bacon, that "usury bringeth the treasure of a realm

into few hands. For the usurer being at certainties, and others at uncertainties, at the end of the game most of the money will be found in the box. And ever the State flourisheth when wealth is more equally spread."

If such be the nature of avarice and usury, is Mr. Bentham justified in releasing them from the restraints of the Usury Laws—laws repealed chiefly through his influence, laws which all nations, ancient and modern, have agreed to institute?   See also Mr. Justice Byles. App. J.

It has been objected against Usury Laws that riches "generally diffused," "liberty of contracts," and the true interest of the borrower and lender afford sufficient protection against usury.

But the general riches of a country can afford none; this history and experience demonstrate. It is, alas! too plain in this present England, that a nation may be rich beyond all parallel, and money abundant, yet whole classes of society reduced to want and despair, lying wholly at the mercy of their creditors.

All this we see and feel this very day.

"'Liberty of contracts,'—what can this avail? Nothing; this is proved by the history of law. For, originally, contracts of loan and interest were unlimited until commerce increased; and with it loans, and with loans multiplied abuses, that brought, by hard experience, every people to impose restraints on 'liberty of contracts' between the debtor driven to borrowing (and 'he who goes a borrowing goes a sorrowing') by urgent necessity, and the monied   Liberty of contracts.

man, who can bide his time, and who knows full well that the fly must ultimately get entangled in his web and yield.

"Does the lender ever inquire whether the borrower is to profit or lose by the loan? Yet there is no honest trade, the average profits of which are 10 per cent., which can borrow money at rates of 10, 15, or 20 per cent., when De Foe (p. 94) shows that even 5 per cent. must entail ruin on the trader, unless he can avoid three contingencies—to sustain no losses, incur no bad debts, and to give no credit." *—*Hannay's* "*Defence of the Usury Laws.*"

Having demonstrated clearly, by the light of history and by reference to daily experience, that usury has been the scourge of all nations, and is, at this day, the crying sin of the times,—that it is inherent in the very nature of metallic money to bring the demands of the monied-man class into existence, it is evident that there is only one remedy: to abjure the precious metals altogether, and to resort to paper money, based on productive labour, and issued by the State.

John Ruskin. John Ruskin has condensed the question in one paragraph; but how many years will elapse before his words of wisdom will be listened to by a people who have given themselves up to a delirium in favour of gold? He writes :—

* Mr. Robert Hannay, in his "Defence of the Usury Laws," ably exposing Mr. Bentham's "Defence of Usury," makes reference to the Usury Laws of all nations, and shows great research ; and his dissection of the Doctrinaires' sophisms is as temperate as it is perfect. "*Defence of the Usury Laws, with a proposal to lower the legal rate of interest to 4 per cent.*" By *Robert Hannay. Blackwood*: 1823.

"The intricacy of the question has been much increased by the hitherto necessary use of marketable commodities, such as gold, silver, salt, shells, etc., to give intrinsic value or beauty to currency ; but the final and best definition of money is, that it is a documentary promise, ratified and guaranteed by the State, to give or find a certain quantity of labour on demand."

Mr. Bentham, being an advocate for gold money, was logically obliged to defend its natural result, usury, but a greater than he had pronounced in favour of representative money—a money without intrinsic value—a paper document deriving all its significance from the signature of a treasury or exchequer official, with the proper stamp, and under the authority of an Act of Parliament. And let it be reiterated that this is no new experiment. We have the example of Pitt's one-pound note before us, with the remarkable results as pointed out by Sir John Sinclair (p. 27). The unfortunate wording of that note, " I promise to pay," gave the bullionists a plausible plea for a return to specie payments. This wording must be avoided in future, and as the specimen given at end of the proposed exchequer note declares, it must only be an engagement on the part of Government to receive it as quittance of taxation, and consequently of debts.

Let all credit, however, be given to Mr. Bentham, whose works on jurisprudence and efforts to reform our law procedures entitle him to national gratitude. It is only when he steps out from the walk in which he stands pre-eminent,

Berkely
versus
Bentham.

"I promise
to pay."
App. K.

and defends the giant injustice which is afflicting all nations—
it is only when he comes forward as a vindicator of a class
who, in this moral civilized Christian country, levy blackmail
on trade and industry, walking among us unpunished and
unabashed, dictating to the State—"a power behind the
throne greater than the throne itself"—bearding and ab-
sorbing the old historic families, crushing the labouring
portion of the nation to the earth, and holding manufacturer
and merchant in thrall;—it is only as the apologist of such
that Mr. Bentham is held up to public animadversion.
How differently must we regard that great man, Bishop
Berkely, who, 150 years since, laid down principles to
guide us to the true philosophy of money in his celebrated
work, "The Querist," a work which our political economists,
including professors, have studiously kept out of sight—
a work declared by John Stuart Mill to be remarkable "for
the strong hold the author has on the fundamental truths,
that the industry of the people is the true source of wealth,
and luxurious expenditure a detriment;" and for the dis-
tinctness with which he perceived, being therein much in
advance of his age, that money is not in itself wealth, but
a set of counters for computing and exchanging wealth, and,
in his own words, "a ticket entitling to power, and fitted to
record and transfer such power."

Bishop Berkely's "Querist."

The *Quarterly Review*, January 1872, even maintains that
Berkely, dwelling on the cause of existing evils, and from
regarding special circumstances from an universal point of
view, had arrived at something approaching a complete

J. S. Mill and the Quarterly on Bishop Berkely.

system of economic science forty years before the appearance of Adam Smith's "Wealth of Nations;" and the *Times*, in a leader chiefly devoted to Ireland, let out inadvertently that "The Querist" contained "more home truths than were ever before or since compiled in so brief a compass,"—which truths expose the folly and injustice of that bullionism of which the *Times* is the sworn champion.

The following quotations from "The Querist" will show that the Bishop's sympathies were not with the usurers, but that he strongly advocates a Paper Money, which, being an instrument that can expand with population and wealth, will never be so scarce as to allow extortionate demands for its use :— *Bishop Berkely's "Querist."*

"Whether money is to be considered as having an intrinsic value, or as being a commodity, a standard, a measure, or a pledge, as is variously suggested by writers ?

"Whether the true idea of money, as such, be not altogether that of a ticket or counter ?

"Whether the terms crown, livre, pounds sterling, etc., are not to be considered as exponents or denominations ? And whether gold, silver, and paper, are not tickets or counters for reckoning, recording, or transferring such denominations ?

"Whether the denominations being retained, although the bullion were gone, things might not nevertheless be rated, bought, and sold—industry promoted, and a circulation of commerce maintained ?

"What makes a wealthy people ? Whether mines of

gold and silver are capable of doing this ? And whether the negroes amid the gold sands of Africa are not poor and destitute ?

" Whether there be any virtue in gold or silver other than as they set people to work and create industry ?

" Whether a view of the ruinous effects of absurd schemes and credit mismanaged, so as to produce gaming and madness, instead of industry, can be any just objection against a national bank, calculated purely to promote industry ?

" Whether a national bank would not at once secure our properties, put an end to usury, facilitate commerce, supply the want of coin, and produce ready payments in all parts of the kingdom ?

" Whether, though the prepossessions in favour of gold and silver have taken deep root, yet the example of our colonies in America (1720) doth not make as plain as daylight that they are not so necessary to the wealth of a nation AS THE VULGAR OF ALL RANKS IMAGINE ?

" Whether our prejudices about gold and silver are not very apt to infect or misguide our judgments and reasonings about the public weal ?

" Whether plenty of all the comforts and necessaries of life be not real wealth ?

" Whether the benefits of a DOMESTIC COMMERCE are sufficiently understood and attended to, and whether the cause thereof be not the narrow and prejudiced way of thinking about gold and silver ? And whether there be any other more easy and unenvied method of increasing the wealth of a people?

"Whether it be not evident that not gold, but industry, causeth a country to flourish? Whether the industry of the people is not the first to be considered as that which constitutes wealth, which makes even land and silver to be wealth, neither of which would have any value but as means and motives to industry?

"Whether in the wastes in America a man might not possess twenty miles square and yet want a dinner or a coat to his back?"

With remarkable inconsistency Mr. Mill, forgetting the praises he bestowed on Bishop Berkely's leading proposition, that money and wealth are quite distinct in their nature, and that money is only a ticket recording wealth, in a later work denounced Paper Money as "a gigantic fraud," and its adoption as "a wholesale confiscation of private property." But not a word do we hear of confiscating the most sacred of all property,—that of a man in his own labour; a confiscation effected by gold money, which has doubled indebtedness. And here one is tempted to quote Mr. Ruskin's pithy apothegm, "Whereas it has been known and declared that the poor have no right to the property of the rich, I wish it also to be known that the rich have no right to the property of the poor."

All legislators, from Moses and Solon up to the present time, have endeavoured, by restricting usury within lawful bounds, to rescue the debtor interest—that is, the great

J. S. Mill praises Bishop Berkely.

All legislators favour the debtor.

mass of the people—from the extortionate claims of the
creditor, or monied interest—claims which, under the calculations of compound interest, may be said to be illimitable ;
but it has been attempted to be shown that metallic money
and usury are inseparable, and that the only remedy is a
documentary instrument issued by the State—a Paper
Money, expanding with population and wealth. `

This attempt Mr. Mill declares to be " one which all true
friends of the people should disavow, as a roundabout
method of cutting down debts to a fraction." Further on
he writes, " That men who are not knaves in their private
dealings, should understand what the word depreciation
means and yet support it, speaks but little for the existing
state of morality, and whether to deliberate on such a question is not as if a private person were to deliberate whether
he should pick a pocket ? "

Deprecia-
tion and
apprecia-
tion.

"Depreciation and cutting down debts." This must
strike the reader as a very one-sided view of the question.
What does Mr. Mill say to *appreciation* and increasing
debts ? And what shall we say of those who, by a sudden
resort to gold payments, made the pound into thirty
shillings, adding by a stroke of the pen one-third to the
burthens of all debtors—those debtors being the men who
find us in food, clothing, lodging, and fuel?

Debt 6000
tons of
gold.

By the Bill of 1817, Sir Robert Peel, backed by Mr.
Horner and the Whigs, by political economists like Mr.
Ricardo, and philosophers, men of the closet, like Mr. Mill,
declared the paper debt to be a debt of 6000 tons of gold,

and this at a time when gold was found hardly sufficient to replace what was consumed by the artificer in wear and tear. "Oh," exclaimed Sir Robert Peel, chucking a sovereign in the air (and this in the House of Commons), "*this is my pound!*" His pound indeed it was, and has inflicted greater wrongs and caused more misery than any other piece of legislation, however wrong-headed. To tie a nation down, whose productive powers, aided as they are by the most wonderful machinery, could double its real wealth every ten years, to a money consisting of the dearest metal known, is a piece of unreason, the consequences of which we see in the social disruption around us.

The orthodox school always assumes that population and production are fixed quantities, instead of being a constantly-increasing factor, requiring more and more circulating medium. "Deprived of this," Bishop Berkely tells us, "the State becomes gouty and inactive." Supplied with this, and, Mr. Hume tells us, "all things assume new life."

Mr. Cobbett was so impressed by the fall of prices incident to the return to cash payments, that he proposed equitable adjustment. In Mr. Mill's eye "this proposal was preferable, seeing it was only knavery, where a depreciated paper was not only knavery but folly; that as great a man as Mr. Attwood declared it to be his creed, that the man who calls two blades of grass into existence where only one grew before, deserves better of his country

Equitable adjustment.

than the whole tribe of statesmen and warriors. Mr. Attwood has the same exalted opinion of the man who calls two pieces of paper into existence where only one existed before."

Surely Mr. Mill would allow the issue of two warehouse warrants in the place of one, if the goods warehoused were doubled.

CHAPTER X.

" Professors, being bound to teach orthodox views, often hinder the progress of truth, as in Galileo's case."

IN the list of political economists whose positions are questioned, Mrs. Marcett and Miss Martineau are placed first, because their books are intended for the young, and are text-books on this subject in schools, besides being generally recommended. This gives them undue importance, for opinions once imbibed in early days, and, it will be a work of immense difficulty to eradicate them afterwards.

Mrs. Marcett on Usury, as to which she apparently has been sitting at the feet of Mr. Bentham, says: "What we now call exorbitant and scandalous usury proceeds in a great measure from prejudice, which prevents the interest of money, like all other pecuniary interests, from finding its natural level, and stamps with criminality and the odium of usury any bargain in which money is lent at a higher interest than 5 per cent., however great the risk incurred by the lender. Why should there be a limit to the terms on which money may be borrowed any more than

8

to the borrowing, or rather, I should say, to the hiring of any other *commodity?*"

Because money is not a commodity, but the instrument which exchanges all commodities; that money is legal tender for debts and taxes (and in nothing else can they be paid). Mrs. Marcett goes on to tell us, that "salt, tobacco, shells, and a great variety of other articles have been used at different times, and in different countries, as a medium of exchange, but nothing has ever been found to answer this end so well as the precious metals."

Of all commodities, metals the best.

Granted, that if money is to be constituted a commodity, the precious metals are to be preferred to all others; but this does not meet the objection of monetary reformers to any and every commodity, because money must be documentary,—an instrument "which by its stamp and signature acquires a local value, becoming as precious and as scarce as gold, and more fit to circulate large sums."—*Berkeley.*

Gold like the trump suit.

Endow gold with the privileges which coining confers upon it, and, like the trump suit in cards, it is invested with supreme power, its lowest number controlling the highest card of the other suits. A man with gold, like the man with a hand of trumps, is sure to win the game.

The daughter in the dialogue asks: "As gold and silver are the standard of value of all other commodities, all other commodities, I conceive, must be affected by an alteration in the exchangeable value of gold."

"And," replies Mrs. Marcett, "this is the reason why

money is not an accurate standard of the value of com- Gold not
an accurate
standard.
modities."

True enough of metallic money, and this the reformers have always maintained.

"Yet," continues the daughter, "what a common obser-vation it is, that plenty of money animates the industry of a country, and encourages commerce; and this seems to have been proved by the miserable and barbarous state of Europe previous to the discovery of the American mines."

Mrs. Marcett answers: "The discovery of America was certainly a very efficient cause in rousing the industry of Europe, but had America possessed no mines, I doubt whether the advantages we have derived from our connec-tion with that country would not have been equally great. We could easily find a substitute for the specie with which she supplies us, but never for the, abundance of sugar, coffee, indigo, etc., she pours upon us."

To this it may be replied, that no possible substitute could Europe have found for the specie with which America supplied her, for this reason, that the nations of Europe, with their worship of gold, had universally agreed Why gold is so that the metal they esteemed so precious should be their precious a metal. only money. This conferred a fictitious value, for no sub-stitute would they tolerate, and their state of civilization rendered the only substitute, a Paper Money issued and guaranteed by the State, impossible, so possessed were the minds of all men with this prejudice. So long as the universal belief in the value of gold exists, so long will the nations prize it above all other commodities.

"Gold and silver, though they have greatly excited the ambition and avarice of mankind, have evidently contributed but little to stimulate their industry."

Australian discoveries. The Australian discoveries did most certainly stimulate the industry not only of this country but of the whole Continent, for the gold was, most of it, coined into sovereigns, adding to our previous stock one hundred millions.

"Were money as liable to variation of value as commodities for which it serves as a medium of exchange, it would be totally unfit for a standard."

This difficulty Sir Robert Peel attempted to meet by coining five dwts., three grains of gold, into a coin which he called the sovereign, and to which he gave a money denomination—twenty shillings. This made the sovereign apparently fixed in value, but the alteration was transferred to commodities, which rose and fell in price as gold became plentiful or scarce. But the sovereign, in which all fixed charges were estimated, made them nominally unalterable, but in actual operation, that is, in purchasing power, those fixed charges became unfixed.

That gold does vary in value, or rather in price, is proved by the rise and fall in discount, which is the price of money. A rate of 10 per cent. indicates a short supply; a rate of 2 per cent. indicates plenty.

For money, however, to rise or fall in purchasing power —and this is the true test by which to try Sir Robert

Peel's legislation—is as injurious, and as subversive of all calculation in the bargains of every-day life, as would be changes in the weight of the pound avoirdupois, which one day might be twenty ounces and the next only twelve.

Caroline justly asks: "Yet is it not a great hardship on the poor to send goods abroad, which many of them are in want of at home ?" *Exporting goods which might be consumed at home.*

Mrs. Marcett: "The poor are first supplied with whatever they can afford to purchase, and without the means to purchase you must recollect there can be no effectual demand."

It did not require a book of 200 pages to tell us that without money the poor cannot buy, but to make demand effectual, money is required. If Mrs. Marcett thought this a sufficient answer to her daughter's very pertinent question, it says little for her powers of reasoning. This is indeed the jargon of the political economist. This, too, in a book which is a popular text-book in schools ; and thus we see the platitudes of the past deeply instilled into the minds of the rising generation.

Miss Martineau has also been engaged, as well as Mrs. Marcett, in misleading the youthful mind and propagating error.

Miss Martineau wrote a child's book also, in which she inculcates the fallacies of the bullionist school, and the following extract from her "History of England" manifests her leaning :— *Miss Martineau on political economy. "History of England."*

"Sir Robert Peel desired to modify the Bank Charter,

and introduced his Bill to the House of Commons in 1844. It was the desire of the country at large that changes should be made, for the last few years had wrought deeply on the public mind in regard to currency matters. The fever of joint stock bank speculation had subsided. Opinions of Mr. Samuel Jones Loyd and Mr. Norman, opinions clearly propounded before a Parliamentary Committee in 1846, in favour of a single source of issue of money, had become widely known and intelligently embraced by a large majority of thinking persons; while, on the other hand, an extensive agitation had gone forward in favour of such an expansion of the currency in all times of pressure as might buy off the pressure, and spread ease through the field of commerce. The intricate and abstract subject of currency had become so interesting to the many, that pamphlets advocating every view had appeared in abundance, and not a few, both of the wise and the foolish, went through several editions. It is easy to understand that some of the most unwise were the most popular.

Miss M.'s admissions. When the small traders and artisans were told *that trade was always good when Paper Money was abundant;* that a new issue of Paper Money had relieved distress as often as it had been tried; and that hardship and misery had always attended a contraction of the currency, it was not surprising that they would read with avidity publications which described the bliss of an abundance of money, and partly consoled them for past misfortunes by appearing to point out the cause of them. Publications more intelligent and more intelligible were read as eagerly as any novel by men of business who were aware that the wisest of us have only too little knowledge and insight on a subject of central interest and importance, a subject on which any man of business would gladly have a clear opinion if he could. On the whole, though the confusion of views was great, and the stragglers were so many as almost to defy calculation, it may be said that there were three parties awaiting the minister's exposition of his views on currency and banking in 1844—the advocates of inconvertible currency of a paper circulation, *open to all comers when desired ;* * the advocates of a legal declaration that paper money was convertible without other safeguard than legal penalties in case of mischievous transgression ; and the advocates of a *real security for such convertibility securely in the form of precious metal* actually laid by under the same roof, from which its representative bank-note goes forth."—*History of England,* vol. ii., p. 624.

The cool assumption and the affected condescension to the ignorance of her opponents are amusing, but the strength of prejudice was never more displayed than in the concession "that it was not surprising, when small traders and artisans were told that Paper Money had relieved distress whenever it was tried, and that misery had always attended a contraction of the currency, that they should read with avidity the publications which showed this plainly and logically."

* "Open to all comers." Is not this an unwarranted misstatement? This was advocated by none.

The surprise is that such a concession as this did not open
Miss Martineau's eyes, who continues:—

Gold and foreign commerce. "It is the portion of our currency which is, or may be,
concerned in our foreign commerce in a department where
our national securities are of no use, and a security must be
provided which is of universal value,—gold."

It is this universal value which utterly unfits gold for
an internal money. Our currency must not be " concerned
in foreign commerce," for foreign commerce is barter—
Foreign trade is barter. manufactured articles in exchange for raw material,—and
even if gold enters into the transaction, it is as a commodity,
and not as a money, for our mint coinage is not recognised
by the foreigner.

Money not meant for foreign trade. The very first essential of a money is, that it shall have
no value in the eyes of other nations, for its prime object is,
that it shall remain at home, to fructify trade, facilitate
exchanges, furnish the till and the purse, pay wages and
housekeeping expenses, and, finally, to give the subject the
wherewithal to pay the taxes the State and the Munici-
pality demand of him. With this documentary instrument
we might dispense with the sovereign; and the whole
coinage might disappear without the slightest inconvenience. France proved this when the Germans abstracted all
her gold (p. 83). It was also proved in Mr. Pitt's time, when
every guinea was withdrawn from circulation, and nothing
but one-pound notes were seen. It must be admitted,
however, that the popular feeling, so used to the sight of
the precious metals, would receive a severe shock on the

introduction of paper; but this was not an insuperable difficulty in 1797.

Miss Martineau pinned her faith on Mr. Samuel Jones Loyd, the reputed author of the Bill of 1844, and who, as such, evidently understood its workings as well as the " cool calculators," for his fortune is computed at several millions.

He it was who declared that under this convertibility, " the Bank of England could only save herself by the destruction of all around her," and whose celebrated cycle gives a graphic summary of its operation on trade.

" The history of what we are in the habit of calling the state of trade is an instructive lesson. We find it subject to various conditions, which are periodically returning; it revolves apparently in an established circle. Thus we find it in a state of quiescence, next improvement, growing confidence, prosperity, excitement, overtrading, convulsion, pressure, stagnation, distress ending again in quiescence." How these oscillations from prosperity one year to stagnation and distress in the next affect trade is shown by extracts from the newspapers of the day. Jones Loyd's cycle. App. L.

Miss Martineau also coincides in opinion with Mr. S. J. Loyd, who is in favour of a " single source of issue." This no one disputes; but the question is, should this single source of issue be entrusted to a private joint stock bank, which has audaciously arrogated to itself the title of Bank of England ? or is it to be a State function, under the control and management of the exchequer ?

Mr. Fawcett, M.P., and Professor of Political Economy in Professor Fawcett.

the University of London, published his "Manual of Political Economy," and it is matter for wonder why he should re-state all the old dogmas of that school, when what he advances has been already better said; for this I have his own confession: "Mr. Mill's work is at once exhaustive and complete."

In Chapter V. the old error is repeated, an error which vitiates all argument built upon it.

Money to possess intrinsic value.

"As a medium of exchange, money should possess an intrinsic value."

If this has not been successfully controverted, this book has been written in vain.

In Chapter VII., "A cursory view may perhaps induce some to believe that the pecuniary loss is inflicted on the home producers of foreign commodities, reduced in price by foreign importation. Such an opinion may be entertained by many, although it indicates a complete ignorance of the principles of international trade." (P. 386.)

Geneva watches cheap.

Let this be tested by the case of Geneva watches—"a foreign commodity." The purchasers of watches, compara-tively a rich class, are benefited by the cheapness; but will Professor Fawcett assert that the watchmakers of London and Liverpool, comparatively a poor class, are benefited by a free trade in watches, which deprives them of employ-ment,—an employment that totally unfits them for turning their hands to anything else ?

German pianos.

This holds good with regard to German pianos, which can be sold in this country at one-third less than Broadwood

can sell them. Certainly a palpable gain to the comparatively rich class who buy pianos; but it will require a
stretch of politico-economical logic to prove this a gain to
any of Broadwood's men, a comparatively poor class.

The poor matchmakers, too, may be cited as a case in
point.

"There can be no right to which a nation has a more *Buy in the
cheapest
market,
and sell
in the
dearest.*
defensible or juster claim, than that every individual of
the community should be freely permitted to obtain commodities where he can buy them on the cheapest terms,
and to sell them where he can realize the highest price."
(P. 387.)

Such are the conclusions to which bullionism leads even
men of such bold thought as Professor Fawcett. Price!
Money Price!! everything is to be weighed in the gold
scales. But are there not things above all price? The
export of coal these political economists view as nationally *In the case
of coal?*
beneficial, because it brings money into the country; but
surely the calculations that one hundred years may see us
at the end of our supplies should give them pause. It is
vain to urge that coal is inexhaustible. Perhaps physically,
yes; but is it commercially? Even now the extraordinary
depths the poor miners have to go appal the imagination.
Another question opens upon us. Is there anything that
France can give us in exchange as valuable to us as coal?

The author was struck at Rotterdam to see the quays *Export of
cattle at
Rotterdam.*
covered with cattle for exportation to England, and the poor
porters of the quay the very pictures of misery and starva-

tion, and yet engaged in taking out of the country food which they could have eaten themselves.

In fact, the political economists devote themselves too exclusively to " WEALTH," as to its modern meaning—gold and silver.

It is bullionism that leads Professor Fawcett astray in treating of foreign commerce.

" We trust that it is now made evident, that it is not the traders or merchants, but the consumers of imported commodities, who derive the greatest benefit from foreign commerce." (P. 386.)

Foreigner chief gainer by free trade.

By the following statement it can be shown that the foreigner is the chief gainer by free trade.

The English farmer, to get a living profit,
     and to pay his rent (the monopoly price
     of the land) and taxes, must get .   .   60 shillings.
But the Californian importer can gain his
     living profit and be enabled to export,
     as is proved by actual prices for recent
     arrivals   43   „
But the competition of free trade compels the
     English farmer to take the market price   46   „
The English farmer is a loser of   .   .   14   „
The American is a gainer of the surplus over
     his living profit of   3   „

The farmer and free trade.

The English consumer is a gainer by the cheapness of corn, but the community consists of the farmer and those under him, as well as the consumers. Another consideration is lost sight of by the political economists. It is a question whether, if England was brought up to garden cultivation, foreign corn would be required—at least for a century.

" But it would not pay."

Certainly not under the gold system; but supply a Land money based on the prospective labour on this inferior soil Tenure. now lying waste, and see if we should not approach to something like garden cultivation. That a bad tenure of land is a hindrance is true, but a proper money would obviate this. Perhaps the political economists will give their attention to this subject, and enforce it on the public mind, for, next to money, land is the most vital question.

If a theory is wrong in principle, it is wrong in all its deductions. The importation of foreign guano, when the native guano, thrown into our rivers, might supply our Native wants, must strike the most casual of observers as a matter for reform. The fine payable to the monied man in the shape of interest on his advances may explain the anomaly, and might not a little protection and encouragement from the State in the way of experiment be advisable, though this proposal must be heresy in the eyes of the disciples of Messrs. Bright and Cobden ?

The Professor is invited to scrutinise the following analysis of profit, and he will see that it is capable of being reduced to its elements—interest of money, or of capital, as it is wrongly called, and wages.

Take a large engineering establishment. There is the Sleeping partner.

Profit is
wages and
interest of
money.

working partner, who brings much experience and skill and practical knowledge, but he brings little money. His share of profit will consist chiefly of wages, and in a lesser degree of interest.

Take a leading shop-keeper in a principal street in London or Liverpool. He receives interest on his money invested on his stock, and he receives wages for his skill in selecting stock, and his daily superintendence and assiduous care. This interest, added to these wages, make up the total of profit.

To go lower in the scale of life. A keeper of a fruit stall in the street has a small capital invested in his apples and pears. His profit is enormous, if we take his capital only into account, but his profit consists chiefly in wages; the care in selecting his fruit and the exposure to the inclemency of the weather must be taken into account.

So, as the chemical analyst brings his sulphuric acid to oxygen and sulphur, must the Professor analyse profit and find that he can eliminate it, and that, disappearing under a distinctive title, it appears again as Interest of Money and Wages, and we have thus the three requisites of production, not as given in Chapter II., "Rent, Profits, and Wages," but as Rent, Interest of Money, and Wages.

This definition of profit would go a good way in clearing the faculties of these unfortunate professors of a science which they have indeed made, owing to their confounding capital and money, a tangled conglomeration of contradiction.

Mr. W. D. Macleod's, of the Temple, is the most recent W. D. Macleod. work, and is entitled " Principles of Economic Philosophy." He has been unable to extricate himself from the groove, and a few extracts will show that he only advances what the old school have been so persistently advocating. He says :

" Small portions of these metals, of definite purity and weight, are manufactured into coins by the State, and a national stamp put on them, to authenticate this purity and weight. In England these coins are called shillings, crowns, sovereigns, and so on. Their true nature then is easy to be understood. They are simply bits of metal, whose weight and purity are attested by the stamp of the State : they are absolutely nothing more."

Absolutely nothing more !—what ! not a money denomination ?

" Why, I ask myself, must a deficiency of gold be regarded as an event more alarming or more disastrous than a short harvest, or a scanty supply of cotton, or scarcity of silk ? "

Because it is legal tender.

" The result I arrive at is simply the demonstration that currency obeys the ordinary laws which belong to all commodities."

Currency or money is not a commodity.

" A nation is not the poorer for possessing little gold, nor the richer for having much : and I earnestly beg you to keep this truth in mind."

If the sovereign is to be the only money, the country is the richer which possesses much gold.

"So says the mercantile theory, and so say the news-papers every day. They hail with delight every arrival of gold from Australia."

And they may well. We may all recollect the fillip given to trade,—the burst of prosperity which attended the Australian discoveries.

But all this mere reiteration of Professor Fawcett and Mr. Mill is answered, and Mr. Macleod may be summarily dismissed.

Professor
B. Price.

Professor Bonamy Price, of Oxford, is the most energetic defender of the gold theory at the present day, and the latest in the field. He opens his work with the appalling announcement, that to commence an investigation of the principles of currency, is to enter a region which may justly be described as chaos. "The very sound of the word currency makes a man turn his back and shut his ears; his immediate instinct is to fly from a subject with which he associates such unendurable jargon." Suppose for the word "currency" we substitute the word "money," and perhaps we may come to some principle that will replace this unendurable jargon by clear and definite ideas.

Currency,
"promises
to pay."

Let us fix in our minds without a doubt that the sovereign is the only money we have in England, and that all currency consists in "promises to pay sovereigns." This clears away a good deal of fog.

The policy of the *Times* has been to discourage all attempts to investigate into first principles, and, with Professor Price, to frighten us all "from looking into the question as one beyond the powers of the human intellect;" but these repeated panics have at last compelled attention to this conventional instrument, a machinery invented by the various nations, for the obvious purpose of giving them the justice of barter, without its inconveniences. May not all this jargon have arisen from a vain attempt to make one commodity a money? May not bullionism be at the root of all this confusion? May we not be the victims of a pre-judice, handed down without question from generation to generation? May not civilization be clamouring for a cir-culating medium capable of expanding with the expanding production created by machinery, and increasing control over the powers of nature revealed to us by chemistry?

The jargon of bullionism.

Lord Overstone must smile when he sees professors of political economy rush forward with so much disinterested zeal to support the principle on which Sir Robert Peel with *his* co-operation founded *his* Bill.

Lord Over-stone.

Is not Bishop Berkely a more disinterested authority than Lord Overstone? and he asks "whether the prejudices in favour of gold and silver are not strong, but whether they are not still prejudices?" And further, "whether paper doth not by its stamp and signature acquire a *local* value, and be-come as precious as gold and silver?" Mark the word *local*, —that money is only valuable to the nation who issues it, and being meant only for internal trade, is not available for foreign commerce. The Professor, however, is quite right when he questions the fitness of bankers and bill-brokers to dogmatise on this question, or esteem as authorities

Money only of local value.

9

great practical City men—men of money. This class is too deeply engaged in the turmoil of daily transactions, too absorbed in details, too busy with sums of money, to study principles of money. They should no more be looked to for guidance than attorneys for enlightenment on the principles of jurisprudence.

Coin only money.

The Professor continues: " Whatever else may or may not be money, coin is at any rate money, and coin is a definite concrete substance (*or, as the vulgar have it, something that rings*). The derivation of the word proclaims this fact, it coming from the word *Monetor*, whose temple was the mint in which Roman coin was made,—the stamped pieces of metal which constituted the currency of Rome. Thus the word money implies minting. Here we are on solid ground," etc.

Romans uncivilized.

Here we are referred for example and instruction to the most barbarous times of a barbarous people, for in the view of true civilization the Romans were barbarians, and this on a question of faith of man in man; but what is this but to tie down with golden fetters the enormous development of production we now see, and to refer us to a time of feebly-developed industry, and to a nation who, under the cursed thirst for gold, attacked and plundered neighbouring nations —for we find them taking city after city, where their first search was for plunder in the shape of treasure, as in the case of Syracuse and Corinth.

Surely the Professor will not adduce as an example these, the greatest brigands, carrying slaughter and fire over the whole known world, and whose unprincipled encroachments in every direction are yet passed without comment by all historians. Credit must have been as incredible to them as it was to M. Esquirol's savage. To him credit or a paper representative was a mere make-believe. Captain Franklin, in his "Overland Expedition," tells us he could not make the Indians of Lake Winnipeg believe that his slip of paper, a draft on Quebec, was really on presentation so many blankets and fowling-pieces. They, like our bullionists at home, did not believe in "filthy rags." M. Esquirol informs us in his "English at Home," that Deerfoot, the Indian runner, was so strict a disciple of his school that "displaying extreme suspicion in matters of self-interest, he for a long time carried about with him all his heavy fortune in gold and silver, unwilling to exchange it even for bank notes, which he considered valueless paper." There are certain fourteen millions of Peel's own issue that, on Deerfoot's principle, are valueless. Deerfoot and Lord Overstone could have hob-nobbed together to his lordship's toast, " In England, gold is our only money."

Mr. Price resumes:—"Every arrival from Australia is hailed with delight in England; manifestly, the country is so much the richer, the money market is so much the stronger. But those who talk in this manner totally forget that gold has to be paid for like everything else."

Why is all this delight ? The reason is plain. Because the law says that this gold is our money, and that it is as indispensable as blood to the body. And this is the excuse for what would otherwise be the absurdity of the mercantile theory—that theory, holding that trade only to be profitable which brings gold and silver into a country encouraged and fostered foreign trade, because there might possibly be balances paid in the precious metals.

Inland trade most important. "The inland or home trade," says Adam Smith, "the most important of all, the trade in which an equal capital affords the greatest revenue and creates the greatest employment to the people of the country, was considered as subsidiary only to foreign trade. It neither, the advocates of the mercantile system averred, brought money into the country, nor carried any out of it. The country could never, therefore, become richer or poorer by means of it, except so far as its prosperity or decay might indirectly influence the state of foreign trade." This idea still pervades the mercantile mind. What congratulations if a few hundred thousands are added to the stock of gold in the Bank of England, and what dismay if as much is abstracted!

As long, then, as this metal is invested with monetary power, so long will its acquisition be looked upon as a matter of life and death.

Mr. Price is landed in strange results in following out this theory :—"Above all, the construction of railways in 1847 had been carried on to an extent far exceeding the savings of the country." The savings, it is to be presumed, taking the shape of gold saved up and deposited in banks.

The stoppage of railways. Now, why were not the railways carried on ? There were the rails and the locomotives ; there were the bricks, slates,

and flags ; lime in abundance ; there were the engineers and
the contractors, all ready and eager to complete the railways; but, above all, there were gangs of industrious, sturdy
men, able and willing at good wages to pile up the embankments and to excavate the cuttings ; and, finally, there was
the food, the lodging, and the clothing for these men. And
why should they not be employed in making these useful
works, instead of being dismissed into compelled idleness
by some occult power that paralyzed their arms, dismissing
them to hunger and privation? This question must be
urgently pressed upon Mr. Price. If the food and the
lodging and the clothing of this army of useful men were
not, by the veto of some mischief-working magician, suddenly in one week annihilated, why should not the work go
on ?—this army, which in one reign covered the country
with a net-work of railways.

Mr. Price gives us the reason why they could not be completed : the magician stands revealed. "The railways could
not be completed by those who had committed themselves
to the shares." Committed themselves to the shares ! This
being interpreted, means that "the shareholders could not
meet their calls." They could not find the money: they
had not the sovereigns. "The resources of the banks were
crippled."

At the hazard of being accused of damnable iteration,
the reader must please bear in mind that the sovereign is our
only money; that bank notes are merely certificates that the
bank has in store sovereigns to honour them when pre-

sented; that convertibility demands that there be no more
notes out than sovereigns in: that bank notes are "promises to pay," and that all bills of exchange, promissory
notes, all currency, *i.e.*, paper running current, is promise to
pay sovereigns. These calls then could not be met. Why?
Because the gold was not there, and the gold being exported or hoarded, the railways were stopped.

Professor
Price on
panic.

To quote Professor Price further :—"The resources of the
banks were crippled.". Those "resources"—what circumlo-
cution have we here ?—were sovereigns of the full weight
and fineness, and they had none, for the fountain head, the
Bank of England, had none. "The shareholders had emptied
out their accounts, and borrowed where they could from the
banks, instead of bringing in deposits. Shares were un-
saleable except at ruinous loss." "Now was the time for the
hard calculator to seize his opportunity, to demand 15 to 20
per cent. for the gold which he has prudently reserved,"
to use the words of the *Times*.

"But the fact to grasp in all this disorder is, that the
shareholders had expended their property in setting
labourers to work, who consumed the wealth and made
diverse constructions on the ground." What wealth had
the labourers consumed ? Why, the bread and potatoes,
the beer and the spirits which were there for them to consume; and Mr. Price will surely concede that, even if
dismissed from their work (useful or useless is not the
question), they must still be fed, and lodged, and clothed.

"Gold, notes, banks, commercial firms are mere machinery;

they are not the wealth of a nation." Mr. Price may call gold machinery if it so pleases him, but it is rather important machinery, if in it only we can pay our debts and taxes.

"But it is true, nevertheless, that the effects of a crisis last for a long time, and this is the great truth to remember, because a crisis is only a culminating point of a long destruction of capital which has preceded." Capital has not been destroyed. A panic ravages no fields, destroys no machinery, burns no mills, blocks up no harbours, trenches up no railways. A panic is a mere rush of all creditors for gold, and the gold, gone or hoarded.

A crisis lasts long.

"Amidst premiums and unlimited markets for stocks and shares, all appeared to be growing rich together (in America), and spent, that is, consumed, goods profusely." The goods were there : why should they not be consumed ? "If a people choose to eat and drink up all their property in one year." This is simply impossible. People can only eat what food there is, and if it is there, why not consume it ? The political economists confound the individual with the nation. An individual may, by getting into debt and not paying, rob his neighbour; but this is impossible with a nation, for the nation consists of creditor as well as debtor. The simple fact stares us in the face, that if food, lodging (houses), and fuel are there, they should be consumed. Why accumulate ? For happiness and comfort consist in the consumption of such necessaries. Mr. Price is thinking of some miser putting sovereigns by in a strong box; but the

Wealth consists of food, clothes, lodging.

present question is about wealth, which our Saxon ancestors properly spelt *wellth,* or all things conducing to well-being.

" A country cannot be well injured by the mere fact that some banks and mercantile houses have been brought to a stoppage."

This is in direct contradiction to his address to the Chamber of Commerce in Liverpool. In this he told his audience :—

Professor Price on panic.

" It makes one shudder to recollect the agonies which convulse trade at these dreadful seasons. The crash of falling houses, the paralysis and distrust which arrest commerce ; the danger hanging over eminent banks and distinguished firms; the difficulty or even impossibility of discount; and these calamities and anxieties revolving in recurring cycles," etc. Here he might have added the consigning hundreds and thousands of labourers and artificers to starvation, the very men who in half a century had made 20,000 miles of railway.

The political economists strenuously advocate accumulation of capital (the old confusion of terms! they mean money), but to what end ? Can a man do more, however great his wealth, than eat, drink, and sleep, cultivate his mind, enjoy the society of his friends ? and does all this require inordinate wealth ? Pope, though only a poet, seems to have arrived at sounder and more truthful convictions than these worthy successors of the philosophers of Laputa :—

" What riches give us, let us now inquire,—
Fire, meat, and clothes. What next? Clothes, meat, and fire,—
Would you have more? Would you more than live?
Alas! 'Tis all that *Rothschild's* wealth can give."

Baron Rothschild's name is substituted, for he is a living Necessaries example how metallic money aids the accumulation of high of life. financiers, and yet even the Baron would find it difficult to eat two dinners or wear two coats; so that with all these elaborate inquiries, we come to the primitive foundation of all wealth—food, lodging, clothing, and fuel. The millionaire can make a palace of his lodging; he can ransack the ends of the earth for all delicacies; he can wear the finest of broadcloth (*nota bene,* he cannot wear two coats or eat two dinners), but it comes after all to food, lodging, and clothing, and the poor "navvie," or agricultural labourer, wants no more; but the Professor upholds a system which deprives him of the common necessaries of life, hurls him to a state of destitution, and, more than all, keeps him idle, stopping his useful work.

Professor Price concludes his "Currency and Banking" with this advice to the people of the United States, warning them of the terrible consequences of paper money, if they should adopt it :—

"A permanently inconvertible currency science pronounces Inconvertible currency to be utterly destitute of justification. The continuance rency of such an indefensible practice in one of the most im- destitute of justification. portant branches of social administration, would place that great nation on a level below the intellectual standard which it has won in the world. Were it to go on, their ⋏

descendants would speak of the want of intelligence it would seem to imply, as the wonderful spot on the great reputation they had inherited.

"The one vital condition for the successful carrying out of this operation is, a general and resolute determination of the American people to have a currency worthy of themselves, and to resume specie payment in earnest."

There is a flavour of bigoted self-complacency in this extract, which is manifested also by Miss Martineau and Mr. Bentham, as if the advocates of different views were objects of pity, as labouring under a delusion, and upholding extravagant and irrational theories.

Accuses
writers of
ignorance.

Amongst other writers, Mr. W. Stanley Jevons has written on "Money and the Mechanism of the Exchanges," which, however, is principally a *réchauffé*, from Adam Smith. In his preface he quotes with approbation Mr. Herbert Spencer, who, in his "Study of Sociology," complains that political science is continually discussed by those "who never laboured at the elementary grammar or the simple arithmetic of the subject." It may be doubted whether Mr. Jevons's work is not a new illustration of the truth of the assertion.

Mr. Jevons knows one gentleman "who holds that exchequer bills are the panacea for the evils of humanity." It is absurd to assert that the issue of exchequer bills would cure any but financial evils, and no one could be bold enough to say that this would be a cure for all the evils of humanity; but it is maintained that paper money based on labour could cure much commercial evil, and this is well put by the late lamented Rector Twells* in his excellent pamphlet previously quoted: "How can paper money increase the wealth of a nation?" a copy of which has been forwarded to Mr. Jevons. In this pamphlet he will find Bishop Berkely, Edmund Burke, David Hume, Benjamin Franklin, Sir Walter Scott, and Sir Archibald Alison brought forward as authorities in favour of paper money.

Mr. Jevons heads his eighteenth chapter, "Want of Elasticity in Paper Money," and proceeds:—"A further objection to a paper money inconvertible into coin is, that it cannot be varied in quantity by the natural action of trade. No one can export or import it like coin, and no one but the Government, or banks authorized by Government, can issue it or cancel it, export or import it." This is to lose sight of a principle, which the bullionist utterly ignores, that it is of the very essence of a money for internal trade that it shall neither be exported nor imported. Mr. Pitt's one-pound note was never exported, for the plain reason that it had no value in the eyes of the foreigner: the sovereign, on the contrary, is often exported, leaving us at home gasping for want of the wherewithal to meet debts and taxes. Moreover, Paper Money can be cancelled.

Advocates export of coin.

John Locke thus illustrates the jealousies, the ill-blood and the struggles between debtors and creditors, when the

---

* "How can Paper Money Increase the Wealth of a Nation?" By the late Rev. John Twells, Rector of Gamston, and Prebend of Lincoln Cathedral.

John Locke on a short supply of money. supply of money is suddenly curtailed. "If one-third of the money," says he, "were locked up (*or exported, as we see in these days*), the people, not perceiving money to be gone, would be jealous one of another, and each would employ his skill and power the best he could to retrieve it again, and bring it back into his pocket in the same plenty as before. But this is but scrambling among ourselves, and helps no more against our wants than the pulling of a short coverlet will, among children that lie together, preserve them all from the cold. Some will starve, unless the father (*the Government*) provide better, and enlarge the scanty covering (*provide more money*)."

Another principle to which Mr. Jevons's attention is invited is, that money, quasi-money, never enters into the account of foreign trade, for this simple reason, that the foreigner does not recognise our sovereign as money. With him it is only a disc of gold of a certified fineness and weight, which certificate he accepts, but altogether without acknowledgment of the money denomination. To the foreigner the king's head and the royal arms on the reverse are nothing. Foreign trade is barter, and even if gold enters into a transaction it is as a commodity simply.

Paper money not drained away. "Some persons have argued that it is well to have a paper money to form a home currency, which cannot be drained away, and will be free from the disturbing influence of foreign trade. But we cannot disconnect home and foreign trade, except by doing away with the latter altogether. If two nations are to trade, the precious metals must form the international medium of exchange, by which a balance of indebtedness is paid." (P. 237.)

If foreign trade is barter, it is an exchange, say, as far as this country is concerned, of manufactures for raw material; as in the case of America, manufactures against raw cotton ; of Brazil, against sugar and coffee; and what balances there are, are settled in gold and silver, as commodities ; and even these balances lie over and are calculated in produce.

Foreign trade is barter.

" Currency is to the science of economy what the squaring of the circle is to geometry, or perpetual motion to mechanics." (P. 237.)

And this will always be the case as long as the wild and barbarous idea is maintained, that gold is to be the favoured commodity—the instrument of exchange for all other commodities.

" Gold and silver, in short, continue to be the real measure of value, and the variable paper currency is only an additional term of comparison which adds confusion."

It is labour, and not gold and silver, which is the measure of value. An American merchant gives three or four bales of cotton for one bale of cotton manufactures, because of the additional labour embodied in the latter.

" There are men who spend their time and fortunes in endeavouring to convince a dull world that poverty can be abolished by the issue of printed bits of paper." (*Preface.*)

Different theories.

It depends upon what authority that paper is issued, and whose signature and stamp may be affixed. The postage stamp is only a bit of gummed paper, but no one regards what the material is as long as its postal power is recognised; a warehouse warrant is only a bit of paper, but its significance and value is derived from the goods warehoused.

"I know one gentleman who holds that exchequer bills are panacea for the evils of humanity."

Exchequer Bills received in payment of customs.

Not exactly so. The gentleman doubtless did not look upon exchequer bills as a cure for the small-pox; but it is a fact, perhaps not known to Mr. Jevons, that exchequer bills are now currency; they are received in payment of customs, but, unfortunately, the sum is restricted to a hundred pounds, and so of little avail for general circulation. Perhaps we may be favoured with a reason why the nation should not make its own credit negotiable, by breaking these notes into small sums, say of one pound, and, if the proposal may not shock Mr. Jevons's nerves, into ten shilling notes, acting on Bishop Berkely's hint, "Whether the principal use of cash be not passing from hand to hand, to answer common occasions of common people, and whether common occasions of all sorts of people are not small ones?"

"Another class of persons have long been indignant, that in this age of free trade, the Mint price of gold should still remain arbitrarily fixed by statute." (*Preface.*)

This fixing the price of gold makes it sometimes the cheapest article the foreigner can take,—consequently, take it he does. Result—gold diminished, the notes are cancelled, and trade suffers syncope from a deficient supply of blood.

"A member of Parliament lately discovered a new grievance, and made his reputation by agitating against the oppressive restrictions on the coinage of silver at the Mint." (*Preface.*)

On coinage of silver.

If it be true according to Bishop Berkeley, that the principal use of cash is for the common occasions of all sorts of people, and that the common occasions of all sorts of people are small ones, Colonel Tomline's proposal is reasonable—more shillings for small shilling transactions.

Colonel Tomline's proposal.

"No wonder so many people are paupers, when there is a deficiency of shillings and sixpences, and when the amount of the rates and taxes paid in a year exceeds the whole sum of money circulating in the kingdom." (*Preface.*)

When everything has to be bought with shillings and sixpences, is it not of vital consequence that there shall be a due supply of shillings and sixpences ? Bishop Berkely asks, " Whether business at fairs and markets is not often at a stand, and hindered, even though the seller has his commodities at hand, and the purchaser his gold, yet for want of change ?" And as silver is only legal tender for forty shillings, the plenty of silver coinage, though convenient for the purse, the till, and for wages, would not affect prices. Mr. Jevons has been too much absorbed in literary pursuits, or he would know that the difficulty of getting silver and small change to pay wages on a Saturday night is exceedingly great.

Bishop Berkely on small money.

The large supply of silver now so complained of in India, would, if coined into rupees, rescue the poor Ryot from the rapacity of the Schroffs.

Both Mr. Jevons and M. Chevalier, who is brought forward as an authority, fail to give a true, full, and explicit definition of money. M. Chevalier defines pieces of money as "ingots, of which the weight and fineness are *Coinage confers a money denomination* certified." This is not full and explicit; he should have added, "and invested with a money denomination." This is the grand function which makes these ingots into money, withdrawing them from the category of commodities. Mr. Jevons's definition is, " Coins are ingots, of which the weight and fineness are certified by the integrity of designs upon the surfaces of the metals." This, too, is imperfect. The sovereign, moreover, is deficient in the primary distinction of a coin, inasmuch as it does not state what its denomination is, namely, a sovereign, or twenty shillings. This is left to be inferred, but surely its distinctive function should be clearly stated on its face.

Gold liable to abrasion A valid objection to gold being chosen is its liability to abrasion. Mr. Lowe confessed in his budget speech, that one-third of the sovereigns were light, and yet on the tax-note there is always attached a warning, "No light gold taken,"—a most serious objection, but passed over in silence.

M. Louis Blanc, in his " History of the Revolution," referring to the assignats, assigns as the particular function of money that it releases us from barter (and gold money is barter) and enables us to effect exchanges with a note of credit. As to his objection that it may be issued ruthlessly and to any amount, this is utterly futile, for the State is to issue it, and to receive it in quittance of taxation, and the State would consequently guard against the depreciation arising from over-issue. As to superabundance from the fecundity of the mines, let us suppose the fecundity too great, and some discoverer should at last come on the matrix !

"Non qu'ils se furent illusion sur les avantages particu-liers attachés à l'emploi des métaux précieux comme inter-médiaires des échanges; ils n'ignoraient certes pas qu'un des inconvénients du papier-monnaie, même lorsqu'il a un gage solide, est de ne pas porter ce gage avec lui partout où il se présente, et qu'un autre de ses inconvénients, plus serieux encore, est de pouvoir se créer à très peu de frais, *presque à volonté*, d'où résulte de la parte des gouvernements une tendance funeste à le multiplier outre mesure, ce qui éntrâme son avilissement et. bouleverse les transactions." Louis
Blanc.

Another French political economist, Jean Baptiste Say, also bears witness to the peculiar benefit derived from paper, in releasing the precious metals from their use in internal trade, and making them available for foreign exchanges. It is also less expensive.

"Tellement qu'une nation qui fait usage d'un papier-monnaie peut employer toute la valeur des métaux que réclaimeraient ses monnaies, à d'autres usages, et n'en jouit pas moins d'un excellent intermédiaire dans toutes ses transactions, sauf peut-être les plus petites. Les métaux Jean
Baptiste
Say.

dont elle n'aurait pas besoin pour ses échanges, servent alors, soit comme utensiles, soit plutôt comme objets d'exportation, et forment une addition à ses capitaux productifs. C'est un avantage que nous apprécierons avec plus de soin lorsque nous étudierons les signes représentatifs de la monnaie et ses autres supplémens."

The extravagant issue of assignats in the French Revolution has thrown back the paper money question fifty years.

Paper Money like Steam.

Paper money, like steam, is a powerful agent for mischief unless under proper control, and however long the nations may struggle under their chains, the time must come when the question of a paper money, expanding with wealth and population, and guaranteed against extravagant issue, must be debated in Parliament, and discussed in scientific congresses and mercantile associations.

M. Louis Blanc, after portraying the enormous evils inflicted on France by the assignat, yet is alive to the objections to metallic money :—

Louis Blanc on Metallic Money.

"Et puis, l'on sentait bien, au fond que les avantages propres au metal ne le rendent préférable au papier que dans un ordre social imparfait, que dans un régime qui, consacrant le séparation des intérêts, se prêtant à leur antagonisme, fait de la défiance l'inevitable contrepoids de la fraude et met à côté de l'impatience de gagner, la peur de perdre ;—oui, c'est justement parce que la monnaie de métal posséde une valeur réelle, parce qu'elle est à la fois marchandise et signe, parce que la faculté de l'étendre ne contrebalance pas celle de la resserrer, c'est justement à cause de tout cela qu'il suffit de l'accaparer pour être maître du mouvement des échanges, c'est à dire de la vie, de l'âme, de la respiration de l'industrie."—" *Histoire de la Revolution*," vol. iv., p. 146.

"Un ordre social imparfait!" in other words, the resort to the metals indicates a low civilization, and indeed it may be a question whether we are sufficiently advanced to avail ourselves of an instrument, pre-supposing great honesty in the government of the nation using it.

There is a great tendency in these days, owing to the profits of trade having been so seriously encroached upon, for men to withdraw from productive works, and to devote themselves to investments in foreign funds, and speculations generally. M. Louis Blanc depicts in lively colours the evils of this perverted activity, and on this topic speaks more reasonably than when descanting on the precious metals :— *Investments.*

"Le jeu de l'agiotage n'est pas précisément illicite, mais il est immoral, et c'est avec justice que les hommes le s'y méprisent, qu'ils refusent leur estime aux égoïstes qu'en font métier. La raison en est simple : c'est que la nation ne gagne rien au déplacement de fortune que l'agiotage peut occasionner ; c'est que l'industrie de l'agioteur ne produit aucun création réelle ; c'est que les capitaux qu'elle emploie son faits pour salarier, pour faire naître des nouvelles productions, ou fabriques des nouveaux ouvrages : en un mot pour servir la société, et non pour être prodigués ou risqués, *Louis Blanc on "Agiotage."*

dans des spéculations frivoles, où l'avantage de celui que
gagne n'est fondé que sur le malheur de celui qui perd, sans
qu'il y ait pour personne aucune autre profit."

Professor Bonamy Price, in a previous page, questions
the fitness of bankers and bill brokers to be esteemed authorities,—questions their authority to dogmatise, because of
their time and attention being absorbed in details, and,
because of their being too deeply engaged in the turmoil of
daily transactions,—in fact, too busy with sums of money
to look into the philosophy of this great factor in the transactions of poor as well as rich.

Mr. John Dun, a Warrington banker, has published a
pamphlet full of most valuable details respecting the position, not only of the Bank of England, but of all the banks
in the United Kingdom. But whilst showing in the clearest
manner the precarious state in which all banking establishments are placed under the present system, he fails to mark
that the leading principle, the key-stone of the Act of 1844,
is to maintain the convertibility of the note.

Mr. Dun has not the courage to give his adhesion to Mr.
Ruskin's idea, that money must be documentary, and that
the question of the future is, "Paper: how and in what
quantity is it to be issued?" Here is the description
of the working of what he still upholds, namely, convertibility :—

"It must be confessed that our monetary system is a very
peculiar one.

"Our whole scheme of credit and banking may be likened

to the familiar peg-top of the schoolboy, which gyrates upon a small metallic point sufficient to support it so long as it spins with rapidity, but inadequate to the task when the rotatory force is relaxed. Credit is the rotatory force of our financial system. So long as this force is unimpaired the system spins merrily on, but when it fails the insufficiency of the small metallic basis becomes only too apparent, and the fabric topples to its fall. Metaphor apart, the case stands thus: bankers hold a certain amount of deposits, which I have estimated at nearly £600,000,000. With part of these they accommodate the customers who discount bills with or take advances from them. Another part—generally a fourth or a third—they hold in Government or other good securities, and in cash at call or short notice with other bankers or bill brokers.

"Such is the development of credit in this country, that it has been roughly calculated that 97 per cent. of the money transactions of the nation are ordinarily effected by cheques, bills, and other expedients."

Such being the case, the wonder is that the mercantile world ever recovers confidence. In fact, it is found that confidence after each panic is slower in reviving and more easily shaken.

"It certainly cannot be good management which brings the leading bank of the kingdom—the pattern bank as it ought to be—periodically to such abject straits that it is only saved from the crowning disgrace of failure by the arbitrary suspension of the law of the land.

" Would not the management of any other joint-stock bank be condemned, if, when a crisis came, it was unable to carry on its business without the assistance of a loan from Government ?"

The Bank of England is here most unjustly blamed, because, under impossible conditions, it breaks down in vain efforts to maintain the convertibility of the note. It is not the bank, but Sir Robert Peel's impracticable theory, that is at the root of all these accusations, recriminations, and captious criticisms.

The Directors are, however, open to the charge of persisting to work this pernicious system without a protest—without a remonstrance—not a symptom of relenting at the anguish and privations of thousands, and blind to the terrible consequences to the nation. A most damning proof of the opposition of their interests to those of the commercial world is afforded by the fact, that in the year 1866, when the country was convulsed by the Gurney panic, they actually declared a dividend of 11½ per cent., as against their usual rate of 10 per cent. They remind us of Charles Lamb's Chinaman, who could only roast his pig by burning his neighbour's house down.

CHAPTER XI.

"There is not enough of food in the country; but the Poor Law enacts that the pauper shall be fed. Who then goes without? The independent workman and the poor ratepayer; the last, moreover, must pay his rates in gold."

THE sophisms of political economists so sedulously inculcated on the rising generation, are now briefly summarised:— Sophisms of political economists.

That currency should vary as it would vary if it were entirely metallic.

That we must beware of having recourse to inferior soils.

That able-bodied paupers must not be employed productively.

That absenteeism is no evil.

That to raise the wages of labour is to impair the fund out of which wages are paid.

That the nation must not be taxed for the benefit of the producing class.

That the consumer must be cared for, but the producer must take care of himself.

That to make a railway is to sink capital.

That money and capital are convertible terms.

That thrift is necessary to increase the capital of a country.

That all commodities should be rendered as cheap as possible.

That emigration should be encouraged, even if it cause the expatriation of skilled artisans, and agricultural labourers.

That taxation on foreign produce falls on the consumer.

That we should buy in the cheapest market, and sell in the dearest, and that we ought accordingly to export coal if a good price is secured.

That gold only being our money, it may yet be allowed to be exported if a profit is secured.

That the colonies should be given up.

So says the strictest sect—the Pharisees of political economy.

"Set the poor to work," says the statute of Elizabeth.

But the political economists have been some time in power, and what have we seen in England and Ireland ? Unemployed poor. The work of the poor taken from them, and given to foreign labourers and foreign artisans. The market which their expenditure would create, no longer an English market, but a foreign one, from which we are shut out.

In both England and Ireland have been erected buildings called workhouses, because no work is to be done there, but which have been more properly called coops, in which the able-bodied and necessitous poor are, on principle, imprisoned and kept idle.

The public must, and do, maintain the able-bodied pauper, but refuse to employ him actively and productively. The public is in the situation of a man who should be bound to pay wages to 1,000 labourers, whether they work or not. Everything which these labourers could produce, would, under the circumstances, be a saving of loss—that is, a pure gain to him.

In the meantime, the numbers of unemployed poor, and the annual value they unproductively consume, fearfully augment. The humble tradesman is ruined by poor-rates. There stand the idle, starving, uneducated paupers, amidst wealth more than fabulous, " an exceeding great army."

A depression of manufacturing or agricultural industry *Danger property.* fills their ranks, and exasperates their discontent. The unemployed poor have already pulled down Government and threatened to destroy property in France; and the danger is not less real here, nor possibly so remote as is generally imagined.

The axiom "Don't cultivate inferior soils," leads to strange *Drainage wanted. App. B.* results. Mr. Mechi tells us that a 100 millions might easily be spent on improving these inferior soils, but they remain in almost a state of nature for want of draining, liming, and manuring. As to draining, a system of arterial drainage, without which all isolated efforts are fruitless, is a mere matter for speculation, for nothing has yet been done. Surely this investment would be better than lending it to foreign nations, who tempt our annuitant class by large and excessive interest, paid for a few years and then repudiated altogether. The land uncultivated and the people unemployed! If metallic money is at the root of this strange state of things, it has much to answer for, and the proposal of Mr. Carlyle (p. 158) seems to point to a remedy,—a remedy, however, utterly impracticable under the demands of the money-lender for interest. The confusion of ideas prevailing as to the difference between capital and money, is owing to a want of definition. If capital be accumulated labour, assisted and augmented by labour now exercised, and if money is a mere conventional instrument adopted by civilized nations to save themselves from the inconveniences of barter, the attempts of the monied men, the *Times*, professors of political economy, and political leaders to confound them, speak somewhat against their powers of reasoning; but Mr. Ruskin is of opinion that ignorance is assumed, and that sinister motives are at work.

Land uncultivated and people unemployed.

Mr. Ruskin thus comments on a pamphlet of the author's:—
" Invest a shilling in the purchase of " Bishop Berkely on Money," being extracts from his " Querist," by James Harvey, Liverpool. At the bottom of the twenty-first page you will find this query, ' Whether the continuous efforts on the part of the *Times*, the *Telegraph*, the *Economist*, the *Daily News*, and the daily newspaper press, and also of monied men generally, to confound money and capital, be the result of ignorance or design ? '

The Times confounds capital and money.

"Of ignorance in great part, doubtless, for 'monied men, generally,' are ignorant enough to believe and assert anything; but it is noticeable that their ignorance always tells on their own side; and the *Times* and *Economist* are now nothing more than passive instruments in their hands. But neither they, nor their organs, would long be able to assert untruths in political economy, if the nominal professors of the science would do their duty in investigation of it. Of whom I now choose, for direct personal challenge, the Professor at Cambridge (Professor Fawcett) ; and, being a Doctor of Laws of his own University, and a Fellow of two colleges in mine, I charge him with having insufficiently investigated the principles of the science he is appointed to teach."—*Fors Clavigera.**

Another sophism, inculcated in their manuals, lectures, and speeches (and even Mr. Gladstone held forth in Hawarden on the advantages of thrift), is, that capital is the result of saving, and that the only way of adding to the capital of a country is to save money. This absurdity is the necessary result of confounding capital and money.

Savings create capital.

So that in their eyes, a working man that can put by an odd ten or twenty or fifty sovereigns, is justified in living in a miserable cottage, so that the rent is low, in clothing his family in rags, and living on garbage; never going to a play or a concert, never buying a picture or a

---

* The author takes credit to himself for making accessible to the many the profound wisdom of the great Bishop, which has, unaccountably, perhaps accountably, been neglected by our professors and writers on political economy.

book, and denying his wife the womanly gratification of dress. The advocates of this wretched penuriousness would find it difficult to separate their favourite virtue, thrift, from the asceticism of the monks, and they apparently lose sight of the consequences on industry and production. Their disciple would be a poor customer to the clothier, the butcher, and—will the teetotalers forgive the suggestion? —the brewer. The bookseller and the artist would be without employment; and as to his cottage, doubtless the jerry-builder would supply him with a cheap and wretched tenement. Theatres, places of amusement, and concerts, might close their doors. This would hold good for all in the higher walks of life, for why should not all exercise this laudable self-denial?

Human nature demands enjoyment.

These doctrinaires must review their doctrine; fortunately, human nature will assert its rights, so that only a wretch will be found here and there to accept their deplorable gospel.

No! The problem of life is to CONSUME MUCH AND PRODUCE MUCH,—to make the most of this planet on which God has placed man to try its capabilities, and test its capacities. Listen to them, and man would revert to the crab-apple and the sloe. He would reject all the gifts that civilization is ready to pour upon him with profusion.

Thrift—accumulation of capital—which, in the eyes of these apostles of the new evangel, is the grand aim of life, is exposed by Mr. Ruskin, the only investigator we have in these days, untrammelled by the stereotyped ideas of the

Mr. Ruskin on accumulation.

schools. He holds up to public scorn, "these accumulators, who, having abundance of this world's goods, more than enough to carry them and their children through life, yet insist upon drawing from those less favoured than themselves, not only enough to live upon extravagantly, but to add considerably to the excessive amount which they already possess. These are worshippers of Mammon, and servants of the devil."*

It is in obedience to these erroneous dogmas that the Poor Law system has been instituted. "Beware of having recourse to inferior soils." Rather than employ the able-bodied paupers in cultivating the nearest common, or draining a bog, keep them in compelled idleness. Import corn and import guano, but let thousands of acres remain undrained, for the ratepayers—already heavily burthened—would not endure the first cost of these improvements, —improvements easily undertaken under the proposed issue. "Don't cultivate inferior soils."

No one can pass a union workhouse without a vague feeling that something must be wrong when such gloomy buildings are required for the housing of the unhappy wretches, whom Mr. Carlyle thus describes:—

"I saw sitting on wooden benches, in front of their bastile and within their ring wall and its railings, some hundred or more of these men. Tall, robust figures, young mostly, or of middle age; of honest countenance, thought- Carlyle on union workhouses.

* Mr. Ruskin's writings are much esteemed in America, and the above quotation is from a broad-sheet which has been circulated by the thousand.

ful, and even intelligent-looking men.   They sat there
by one another, but in a kind of torpor, especially in a
silence which was very striking.   In silence, for, alas, what
word was to be said ?   An earth all round crying—Come
and till me, come and reap me; yet we sit here enchanted !
In the eyes and brows of these men hung the gloomiest
expression, not of anger, but of grief, shame, and manifold
inarticulate distress and weariness; they returned my glance
with a glance that seemed to say, ' Do not look at us.   We
sit enchanted here ; we know not why.   The sun shines,
and the earth calls; and by the governing powers and
impotences of England we are forbidden to obey.   It is impossible, they tell us.'   There was something that reminded
me of Dante's Hell in the look of all this; and I rode
swiftly away."—"*Picturesque Tourist,*" *quoted by Carlyle.*

Proposal
as to
pauperism.

Mr. Carlyle proposes a most effectual remedy, but Sir
Robert Peel's Bill stops the way to this or any other proposal requiring outlay :—

" My own sad conviction is, that before either paupers
can be dealt with, or waste lands and colonies got to turn
out other than infatuations and futilities for them, Government must do the most original thing proposed to it in these
times,—admit that paupers are really slaves, and fallen
into disfranchisement, who cannot keep themselves free,
and whom it is bitter mockery and miserable folly and
cruelty to treat as what they are not, and accordingly must
take command of said paupers applying for the means of
existence, and enlist them, and have industrial colonels,

first one, and then evermore; and lead and order and compel Industrial colonels. them, under law as just as Rhodamanthus, and as stern, too; and on the whole must prosecute this business as the vitallest of all, and develop it evermore, year after year, and age after age; and understand anywhere, that its industrial, not its red-coated fighting one, is to be the grand institution for the time coming. What mountains of impediment, —what blank, weltering, abominable oceans of unveracity of every kind, the complete achievement of this problem (in the gradual course of centuries) now supposes the annihilation of; all this, alas! is too clear to me. But all this, as I compute, must actually be done, whether before we have ' Red Republic ' and universal social dissolution, or after it; that is now the practical question, and one of the most important the English nation ever had before it. To see such a problem in any form begun, would be an unspeakable relief; like the emergence of solid land again, amid these universal deluges of revolution and delirium."

Such is Mr. Carlyle's remedy; but here we have to face Impracticable without paper money. the old difficulty.

The capitalist would have to be called upon for advances, and would demand interest, a further burden on the taxpayer. But the remedy, an issue based on the prospective labour of the paupers, is scouted by the political economists, and in this Mr. Carlyle is in agreement with the disciples of the dismal science. In fact, he seems to entertain a hearty repugnance to the money question,—a repugnance which mars his usefulness, for " safety lies that way."

The very first step to be taken would be the purchase of the land ; afterwards draining, fencing, and manuring would have to be paid for; and finally, the paupers employed on this land must have wages, if any effectual work is to be got from them. All this requires money. Are the parishes to borrow money at 5 per cent., and to burthen themselves and all posterity with interest—interest which in twenty years would cover the capital ?

Mr. Carlyle, however, is on the right track, and if ever we are to head pauperism, some such plan must be adopted.

A remedy for this pauperism—this cancer in the body politic—is proposed by Mr. Martin H. Boon, one of the most intelligent of the leaders of the working men, and secretary to a society for the encouragement of home cultivation, who thus illustrates the necessity of a paper money if any effectual steps are to be taken to take inferior soils into cultivation. Let such an obvious policy be adopted, and a wide field of employment is opened for these helpless, wretched men :—

Martin H. Boon on Representative Money.

" I am aware that many will say, Is it your intention, then, to make money ? To this question I will decidedly answer, Yes, the same to be redeemed by the co-operator on the farms as previously stated. And it must be remembered that this representative money, so created, would not only be the means of giving the opportunity to the 1,920,000 men to work on our untilled land, producing large quantities of wheat, but also give employment to builders, agricultural implement makers, furniture makers, and, in fact,

to all who are employed in any way making the necessaries
and conveniences of life. And let it not be forgotten that
this money would eventually find its way into the hands
of the surveyors and contractors, who would be able to
employ a large number of navvies, carpenters, bricklayers,
iron-workers, and other mechanics, for making supplemen-
tary railways, as feeders to our large termini, and thus
open up all districts throughout the country, bringing about
a closer union between the citizen and peasant : also, in
making waterworks that would supply our towns with
pure water—cutting irrigating canals throughout the length
of the land, so that when we have hot and dry summers
the crops should not suffer and the supply fall short: making
subways and sewers in all our towns, and erecting establishments to receive the excrements of our cities, to be
converted into deodorised guano : making embankments to
all our rivers, so as to utilize the mudbanks, which at the
present time only create fever and pestilence : pulling down
the worst parts of our towns, and rebuilding them on a good
sanitary system : building large schools, with playgrounds
attached ; and houses with all the latest domestic accommodation for our working classes, the producers of all our
wealth : also in making cheap trains and railways to carry
lime, clay, sand, and the rich alluvial soil of our river beds
to the poor, bog, fen, and moor lands, wherever situated.
Men being employed on these useful works would be the
means of increasing trade throughout the country, which
would bring prosperity to all."

11

This proposal of home colonization is in direct opposition to the teachings of these present dictators of our social policy, as will be evident from their leading dogma, " Don't cultivate inferior soils."

Historians neglect finance. A popular work has lately appeared, which has been largely adopted in schools, "A History of the English People," by the Rev. J. Green, in which there is not the slightest allusion to the financial policy of Mr. Pitt, in 1793, when he passed the Bank Restriction Act, nor any reference to the important effect on the prosperity of the country by Sir Robert Peel's reversal of that policy. The author is apparently totally unconscious of the immense influence such changes have on the public weal. Another "History of England," epitomised from Hume, and intended for students, passes over the subject without comment.

Finance will be proved to be the keystone of history, and historians will be compelled to bring it more prominently before students. The issue of paper money on the cultivation of land is described by Rector Twells in his pamphlet (page 60), as is the effect in the time of Napoleon by Sir John Sinclair (page 28); but the restoration of Frederick the Great. Silesia by Frederick the Great is less known, and his success in raising Prussia from a state of prostration after exhaustion by war, illustrates its advantages forcibly:— That wise monarch issued land-mortgage notes, called *Pfenbriefe*, bearing interest, but inconvertible so long as the interest was paid. With these monetary instruments he forced or fostered Prussian agriculture, and caused it to grow in strength and riches beyond any country in the world, except the United States. The Pfenbriefe were so good a security that they were readily negotiable, even during all the wars of Napoleon.

Again, take the case of Scotland, as stated by Sir Walter Scott, in his *Malachi Malagrowther's Letters,** to show how the wealth of a nation is increased by paper money. " I assume," says he, "without hazard of contradiction, that banks have existed in Scotland for near one hundred and twenty years—that they have flourished, and the country has flourished with them—and that, during the last fifty years particularly, provincial banks, or branches of the chartered banks, have gradually extended themselves in almost every lowland district in Scotland ; that the notes, and especially the small notes, which they distribute, entirely supply the demand for a medium of currency ; and that the system has so completely expelled gold from the country of Scotland, that you never by any chance espy a guinea there, unless in the purse of an accidental stranger, or in the coffers of these banks themselves. This is granting the facts of the case as broadly as can be asked.

" It is not less unquestionable, that the consequences of this banking system as conducted in Scotland, have been attended with the greatest advantage to the country. The facility which it has afforded to the industrious and enterprising agriculturist or manufacturer, as well as to the

Sir Walter Scott.

"Malachi Mala-growther.".

---

* The author recollects these letters coming out in the old *Globe and Traveller*, now fifty years since.

trustees of the public in executing national works, has converted Scotland from a poor, miserable, and barren country,
into one where, if nature has done less, art and industry
have done more than in perhaps any country in Europe,
England herself not excepted. Through means of the
credit which this system has afforded, roads have been
made, bridges built, and canals dug, opening up to re-
ciprocal communication the most sequestered districts of
the country,— manufactures have been established, un-
equalled in extent or success,—wastes have been converted
into productive farms,—the productions of the earth for
human use have been multiplied twenty-fold,—while the
wealth of the rich, and the comforts of the poor, have been
extended in like proportion. And all this in a country
where the rigour of the climate, and the sterility of the
soil, seem united to set improvement at defiance. Let those
who remember Scotland forty years since bear witness if I
speak truth or falsehood."

Sir Walter Scott's letters had the effect of preventing the
withdrawal of one-pound notes from Scotland.

Take another *fact* as to what paper money has effected
on a smaller scale in more recent times, as described by that
able writer and eloquent advocate, Jonathan Duncan :—

The
Guernsey
Market.
"The States of Guernsey, having determined to build a
Meat Market, voted £4,000 to defray the cost. The notes
were guaranteed by the whole of the property of the Island,
said to be worth four millions. These notes did not bear
any interest, nor were they convertible into the precious

metals. They were tokens, not possessing any intrinsic value, but only that conventional or representative value which they received from the authority of the States by which they were issued. They were the symbols of the *real money* of the Island. They were worthless to any other community than Guernsey, and therefore there was no inducement to their exportation. Consequently they remained permanently in local circulation for local purposes. They were inscribed ' Guernsey Meat Market Notes,' and numbered from 1 to 4,000, each note representing £1 of account in the currency of the Island. They were legal by universal assent. With these notes the States paid the contractor; and with them he paid his workmen and all who supplied him with materials. They were freely taken by tradesmen for goods, by landlords for rent, by the authorities for taxes.

" In due season the market was completed. The butchers' stalls, with some public rooms constructed over them, were let for an annual rent of £400. At the expiration of the first year of this tenancy, the States called in the first batch of notes, numbered 1 to 400, and with the £400 of real money received for rent, redeemed the £400 of representative money, expressed by the ' Meat Market Notes.' At the end of ten years, all the notes were redeemed through the application of ten years' rental; and since that period the Meat Market has returned a clear annual revenue to the States, and continues to afford accommodation, without having cost a farthing in taxes to any inhabitant."

Can it be doubted that, as this able writer infers, the system which enabled the States of Guernsey to build their Market, would, if the restrictions on the issue of Representative Money were removed, develope the resources of the whole kingdom ?

If the principle is sound, we can apply it to every contingency of life. Emigration, the cause[of so much suffering and privation, might be deprived of half its horrors if the poor emigrants were supplied with advances on their future labours, in order to provide them with passage-money, and outfit.

Supply emigrants with outfit,

This is the proper place to protest against the absurd plan of sending off troops of young girls, under the care, too often proving totally inefficient, of a matron.

The position is demoralising for all parties, and Edward Gibbon Wakefield's suggestion should be systematically carried out. The emigration fund, he proposes, should be limited to the sending out of young married couples only; no unmarried youth or girl, nor children, and no aged people, —only young married couples. It would be found that this condition would readily be complied with by the youths and maidens, and the principle of increase transferred from the old country to the new.

Young married couples only to be assisted.

Each girl would then have her natural protector, and the immorality, now too prevalent in these female emigrant ships, be stopped. The proposal then is to issue paper, based on the prospective labour of these young married couples. Find them in one year's subsistence and in tools.

and in a wooden house. If it was generally known how poor emigrants are victimised by usurers and rascally money dealers, this proposal would meet universal approval. Nothing is more common than for the poor immigrant to find his growing crops seized by the ruthless money scrivener, who, taking him at an advantage, before he can house his crop and stack his corn, seizes his land, with the improvements, for interest on advances, and sends him off heart-broken to begin the world again.

"Of course, the advocates of paper money, as an instrument of exchange which would keep pace with production, see no use in sending people—the bones and sinews of the nation —abroad, when we could employ them at home, making over-population balance over-production; but as there might still be adventurous spirits who would like to try their fortunes under the new conditions of cheap land and light taxation, paper money might be issued, based on the future labour of the emigrants, each of whom should leave the country with a hundred pounds in exchequer notes of twenty or even ten shillings each—imperial legal tender— in his pocket. £100 advanced.

"Paris was improved and beautified so as to be an object to visitors from all parts of the world; in fact, they seem to manage things better in France than we do, with all our boasted superiority, as this short instance will show:— Paris improved.

"'Two hundred thousand men have been employed through the winter on the improvements in Paris, and owing to the fine weather have hardly lost a day.'—*Times Paris Letter*, August 8th, 1864.

"To it Wellington owed his successes in the Peninsular War.

"Mr. Pitt issued one-pound notes, and with these the internal trade of the country was carried on, enabling the Government to send all the guineas to the Duke of Welling-ton, then engaged in the Peninsular campaign. The Duke paid his way with guineas, whilst Soult robbed and plundered. The Spanish population were roused to resistance by the depredations of the French marshal, whilst Wellington's army was well supplied. Even when the Pyrenees were crossed, and the British troops were advancing on Thoulouse, their camp was frequented by the French peasantry and farmers, who avoided their plundering countrymen."—*J. Harvey's "Exchequer Note versus the Sovereign."*

Duke of Wellington in Spain.

We have repeatedly approximated in this country to a Representative Paper Money, and nothing but the ignorance of the people of money's real value and use has prevented us from deriving the greatest advantages from it. An instance is given by Lord Macaulay, in his "History of England" (vol. iv., p. 628).

Exchequer Notes in 1696. App. P.

"Another, and at that conjuncture (1696) more effectual substitute for a metallic currency, owed its existence to the ingenuity of Charles Montague. He had succeeded in engrafting on Harley's Land Bank Bill a clause which empowered the Government to issue negotiable paper at the rate of threepence a day in a hundred pounds. In the midst of the general distress and confusion appeared the first exchequer bills, drawn for various amounts, from a hundred pounds *down to five pounds.* These instruments were rapidly distributed over the kingdom by the post, and were everywhere welcome. The Jacobites talked violently against them in every coffee-house, and wrote much detestable verse against them, but to little purpose. The success of the plan was such that the Ministry *resolved at one time* to issue *twenty-shilling bills,* and *even fifteen-shilling bills,* for the payment of the troops. But it does not appear that this resolution was carried into effect. It is difficult to imagine how without exchequer bills the Government of the country could have been carried on during that year."

Lord Macaulay, after this admission as to the utility of excheqer notes, alludes slightly to another important topic, Mr. Harley's Land Bank Bill, by which landed proprietors might have made land negotiable. This Bill was evidently designed to rescue the landed interest from their thraldom to the City magnates. Its defeat was owing to the machinations of the Whig Cabinet—always in close alliance with these "hard calculators." Yarranton shows the straits the landed gentry were in in those days, as they are indeed in these, for want of such accommodation.*

Mr. Harley's Land Bank Bill.

At the same time the Bank of England was founded,—a mere joint stock company, which, by boldly assuming this name, imposed on the people, assuming a power which no Government should permit to pass from its own hands.

Bank of England usurpation.

* See Yarranton's "Appeal" in Charles II.'s reign, App. Q.

This corporation, whose chief care is to see 10 per cent. divided among its shareholders, does not hesitate " to sacrifice all around her," and when unable to pay her way, audaciously demands from the Minister of the day a licence to issue inconvertible paper.

Exchequer
Bill. App.
R.

Further on we are told that exchequer bills were issued as low as five pounds. This was rescinded, for at the present day no exchequer bills are issued lower than £100, and to this is appended an extraordinary and totally uncalled-for boon to the holders, namely, interest at the rate of threepence a day, which is nearly 4 per cent. a year. Nothing shows the ignorance and carelessness of the House of Commons more than this—that House whose prime function it ought to be to watch over the public purse. If it paid the slightest attention to such a question, it would see the folly of a nation paying interest on its own credit. What better

Exchequer
Notes of
one pound.

money could we have than these same notes, brought down to one pound, or even ten shillings?

That prosperity and flourishing trade are the sure concomi-

Marco
Polo.

tants of an expansive currency is testified by Marco Polo, in his interesting account of his embassies in China in the 15th century. He passes from one flourishing city to another, where the industry of the people, and the luxurious style of living among the mandarins and the nobles, fill him with continual surprise. His concluding comment on leaving each city is, " The paper money of the Grand Khan is current here."

The following extract from Mr. Marsden's translation gives the following description of the great city of Kinsai:—

"Upon leaving Via Giu, you pass, in the course of three days' journey, many towns, castles, and villages, all of them well-inhabited and opulent. The people are idolaters, and the subjects of the Grand Khan. At the end of three days you reach the noble and magnificent city of Kinsai, a name that signifies the celestial city, and which it merits from its pre-eminence to all others in the world in point of grandeur and beauty, as well as from its abundant delights, which might lead an inhabitant to imagine himself in Paradise. Rich and populous cities in China.

"Singan is a large magnificent city, the circumference of which is twenty miles. The inhabitants are idolaters, subjects of the Grand Khan, and use his paper money.

"Departing from Chan-ghian-fui, you pass many towns and fortified places, the inhabitants of which are idolaters, live by art and commerce, are the subjects of the Grand Khan, and use his paper money. The necessaries of life are here in plenty, and the variety of game affords excellent sport. Paper money issued by the Grand Khan. App. S.

"Sa-Yanfu is a considerable city. It is a place of great commerce and extensive manufactories. The inhabitants burn the bodies of their dead, and are idolaters. They are the subjects of his Majesty, and use his paper currency."

Other cities are mentioned, and the use of paper money, if not always mentioned, is implied.

The particulars of the fabrication of this paper money, and the ceremonies used in its issue, and the formalities of stamping and signature by the principal officers of the financial department are given in Appendix S.

CHAPTER XII.

" Men put an imposition on themselves when they talk of bequeathing property. They only leave a musty parchment, by which, as a patent, to extort
from their neighbours what the labours of their neighbours have produced."—
GODWIN.

Railway
earth-
works and
labour.

THIS insane delusion that possesses the nations, that no
railway can be made without gold, that this now necessary work cannot be commenced in a new country without
a loan of gold from the capitalists of London, may perhaps
be dispelled when they ask themselves " What is required
in the construction of a railway ? " Labour is the first
requirement—labourers to dig cuttings, raise the embankments, and build the stations; and while so employed they
must be fed, lodged, and clothed.

As the land may be had for little or nothing, the raw
material is lying at hand in abundance.

Then the engineer—generally an Englishman or a Scotch-
man—with his staff, must be engaged. His salary consists
of the produce of the country.

Then the rails and the locomotives, which the English
manufacturer will supply.

Now, here we have the country itself supplying the labour
and the raw material, to pay for which the Government

might issue a paper money; but the locomotives and the rails are foreign products, and under the present system must be paid for in gold. But this is unnecessary. The payment ultimately resolves itself into the products of the country— so much cotton, coffee, sugar, hides, drugs, etc., for so many locomotives and rails.

So that the railway, like the Guernsey market (p. 164), might be made without an ounce of gold being required. Guernsey Market.

The question of a railway then resolves itself into the mere ability of the country to find food, clothing, and lodging for the labourers; to find clay, lime, shingles, flagging, and timber, and to grow the produce of the country in sufficient abundance to export it in exchange for the locomotives and the rails.

In fact, such an expedient was resorted to by Mr. Stephenson in carrying the London and North-Western Railway over Shap Fells, a wild and unpeopled district. He established the much-abused truck system; that is, by an organised supply, he rescued the navvies from the exorbitant exactions of the hucksters and sutlers, and brought the necessaries of life to the doors of their shanties, and this at reasonable prices; for no one will suppose the London and North-Western Railway would take advantage of the necessities of their industrious workers to charge *huckster* prices. Mr. Stephenson then, under the authority of the Directors, issued tickets, which passed current at the stores, and in fact were received without question by the radesmen in the country round.

A plan has been proposed by the Liverpool Currency Reform Association, which, as a preliminary step to a more perfect system, might be advantageously adopted, a plan which finds favour in America, where many, alive to the imperfections of the present system, long ardently for a change.

Consol Notes proposed.—" A plan of Currency Reform has been promulgated by the Liverpool Currency Reform Association, which, as an immediate step, might be adopted with advantage, and which would certainly be a vast improvement on the Act of 1844. The plan is to give all holders of consols permission to deposit their certificates, thereby annulling their claim to the 3½ per cent., and receiving in return legal-tender notes, with further power, if they choose, to pay in again those legal-tender notes, and then resume their character as fundholders. This plan must go for what it is worth. The tendency of such a measure would be to keep money always at 3½ per cent., which is too high; still, the enormous fluctuations in the rate of discount under which we now suffer would be done away with."

—*J. Harvey's " Exchequer Note versus the Sovereign."*

This plan of making National Debts negotiable, is strongly advocated by the American Reformers. The exchequer note is certificate of floating debt, which is not issued under £100, and as the Exchequer pays the holder 3½d. per day, it is a favourite investment with the frequenters of the Stock Exchange. But why should the nation pay interest on its own credit, when these very notes, if reduced into one-pound notes, might serve as a

Liverpool plan, consol notes.

Exchequer Notes.

useful medium in which the subject might pay his taxes? In fact, as has been stated previously, they now are used in their present large amounts by merchants to pay customs, and by manufacturers to pay excise; but so large a sum as £100 can be little available as a general rule, whereas the circulation of one-pound notes would revive trade, and the nation would save the bonus now monopolised by the capitalists in the City.

Customs payable in exchequer notes.

Whilst on the subject of one-pound notes, attention must be drawn to the stringent effect of the law of 1844, which restricts the issue of any note of a less amount than five pounds. The animus of this is very evident. It is carrying out Sir Robert Peel's theory, that money must not be too plentiful. The five-pound note can only be used in the large payments of the capitalist; it is perfectly unavailable for the payment of wages, for the till of the small shopkeeper, or for the every-day demands on the purse. This absurd restriction might surely be removed, and this without trenching on their darling theory, the very keystone of their system—the inconvertibility of the note. Issue five millions of one-pound notes in the place of one million of five-pound notes, and the effects would be beneficial and immediate. Small money is more widely useful than large. Bishop Berkely was well aware of this, for in his "Querist" he asks,—

Five millions of £1 notes instead of one million £5 notes.

" Whether silver and small money be not that which circulates quickest and passeth through all hands, on the road, in the market, at the shop ?

"Whether, all things considered, it would not be better for a kingdom that its cash consisted of half a million in small silver than of five times that sum in gold?

"Whether there be not every day five hundred lesser payments made for one that requires gold?

"Whether the principal use of cash be not the passing from hand to hand, to answer common occasions of the common people, and whether common occasions of all sorts of people are not small ones?

"Whether business at fairs and markets is not often at a stand and hindered, even though the seller hath his commodities at hand, and the purchaser his gold, yet for want of change?

"Whether, as wealth is really power, and coin a ticket conveying that power, those tickets which are fittest for that use might not be preferred?

"Whether those tickets which singly transfer small shares of power, and, being multiplied, large shares, are not fitter for common use than those which singly transfer large shares?

"Whether the public is not more benefited by a shilling that circulates than by a pound that lies dead?

"Whether sixpence twice paid be not as good as a shilling once paid?

"Whether the same shilling circulating in a village may not supply one man with bread, another with stockings, a third with a knife, a fourth with paper, a fifth with nails, and so answer many wants which otherwise must have remained unsatisfied?

" Whether it be not the industry of common people that feeds the State, and whether it be possible to keep this industry alive without small money?"

Though these queries refer to the advantages of small change, yet the proposed substitution of one-pound notes is the same principle carried out—a principle that would vindicate the propriety of issuing ten-shilling notes—notes facilitating, as they would do, the daily exchanges "answering the common occasions of common people."

Mr. Girdlestone, of Weston-super-mare, whose pamphlet Mr. Ruskin declares to be the most complete and logical statement of economic truth that he has ever seen in the English language, thus states the case of the man whose income arises from the rents of land or houses which he has inherited, and he asks, " What shall we call him ? "

E. D. Girdlestone on bequests.

" Here is their history. The patriarch aforesaid, imagining that a wholly idle life must be a very desirable and honourable one, and preferring naturally the interests of his own children to those of other people's children, determined, by settling his property on his posterity, or at any rate bequeathing it to them exclusively, to put them at ease for all future time. He compassionated them; he felt for them, as we do for the beggar in the street. His prophetic eye discerned a long line of unborn generations of descendants on their knees before him, begging, and on his deathbed he entailed his property on them.

Bequeathment a lien on future labour.

" Though the descendants of such a man are not living by work of their own, they are living by work, for they are

12

living by their ancestor's work. I reply by denying *in
toto* the doctrine of imputed industry or of vicarious industry."—"*Society Classified.*"   *By E. D. Girdlestone, B.A.*

High rate
of interest
a premium
on idleness.
High rates of interest of money act as an inducement to
men to leave the pursuits of industry, and to retire, as it is
called, that is, join that large body of annuitants or people
living on income. The home-fund holder and the foreign
dividend receiver, the owner of gas shares and joint stock
banks and railways, form a large body of idlers, who devote
their lives to foreign travel and to the cultivation of dilettante tastes, and are an unmitigated burthen on labour and
industry.

Interest of
money.
Let our millionaires and high financiers, our dabblers in
stocks, investers in foreign loans, and "watchers of the
turn of the market," bear in mind that the question of
INTEREST OF MONEY must undergo investigation. Why
should labour have to pay £150,000,000 a year for the
use of an instrument which should come into existence as
the shadow follows the substance ? What is this living on
" vicarious industry," as Mr. Girdlestone calls it, this reliance
on scrip, mortgage, or title-deeds—this lien on productive
labour, but living on false pretences ? Let Mr. Ruskin's
definition be admitted, and usury, the offspring of scarce
money, will disappear :—

Mr.
Ruskin's
definition
of money.
" The intricacy of the question has been much increased
by the hitherto necessary use of marketable commodities,
such as gold, silver, salt, shells, etc., to give intrinsic value
and security to currency; but the final and best definition

of money is, that it is a documentary promise, ratified and guaranteed by the nation, to give or find a certain quantity of labour, or the results of labour." Proudhon.

The propertied classes must look into this question of Interest, if they wish to suppress socialism and republicanism, and theories such as Proudhon's apothegm, "La propriété c'est le vol."—"The land of England belongs to the people of England."—"The duty of Government to employ all men out of work."

And the workers—when will they rise to a just apprehension of this great injustice—this "Old Man of the Island," who is riding them to death? When will they make an intelligent demand for enfranchisement—intelligent, methodical, and organised? All this is a long way off, but let us trust in truth and its power. God has endowed man with reason, in order to fit him for truth—for embracing it when intelligibly and clearly laid before him, and embracing it with ardour and enthusiasm. Let them not look for assistance from the middle classes, unless it be here and there that a man, earnest and wise, who, refusing to measure great social questions by the foot-rule of his own private petty interests, will stand up for the right, and advocate the true ; and there are such men even now, and will soon be more. But as a class, the propertied and the middle ranks of life will imagine that their interests will suffer, and will therefore defend their coupons, shares, debentures, and mortgages à l'outrance. Their organs, the *Times* the *Telegraph*, the *Daily News*, the *Economist*, with the No assistance from middle class.

From the press. App. A.

provincial papers at their back, try to envelope the
question in fog, and persistently inculcate that falsest of
dogmas, that capital and money are synonyms—that they
mean the same thing, and are convertible terms.   Little
From the pulpit. assistance is to be looked for from the pulpit; the ministers
of religion hold aloof, for they know to whom they must
look for contributions and subscriptions, for stipend and
support.   (Public worship is a middle class institution, and
the pew rents, and the organised system of begging carried on, deter the working men, for they have no money
From Politicians. to spare) :—no help from political leaders, who give all
their energies to party questions; and if indeed this question
of Interest became prominent, the wealthy Liberal leaders
would secede, and join the Conservative ranks:—one would
From Professors of political economy. expect the professors of political economy would come to
the rescue; but no, they are too busy teaching the cate-
chism of bullionism.

Let not, however, the advocates of the money of civilization bate one jot of heart and hope; but persevere in incul-
cating principles, unpopular only because not understood.

This brings us to the consideration of the common ideas
Succession. which prevail on the succession to estates, and the descent
of property by will,—ideas resulting from ill-defined notions
as to the source of all wealth.   What would be the value of
an estate, though handed through a dozen generations, if
there were not men to cultivate, and farmers to superintend
and direct their labours ?   This property, so handed down, is
the creation of law, which by parchment ratifies possession.

This is true of those endowments so profusely spread over the country. There was lately much discussion of the rights of the "pious founder," and whether the living generation could interfere with the capricious and often absurd stipulations annexed to these charitable legacies. Without going into the question of motives of pure philanthropy, personal vanity, or a jealousy of expectant heirs, a slight examination will show that the "*pious founder*" was leaving nothing behind him but a mortgage on the labours of generations unborn. Godwin puts this clearly in his "Political Justice." " Pious founders.'

"It is a great imposition men are apt to put on themselves, when they talk of the property bequeathed by their ancestors, that property being produced by the daily labour of men now in existence. All that their ancestors bequeathed to them was a mouldy patent by which, as a title, to extort from their neighbours what the labours of those neighbours had produced."—*Godwin's " Political Justice."* Godwin.

To illustrate this, let us take the estates which, in 1724, Thomas Guy left to found his hospital. We need not go into the questionable manner in which he accumulated his wealth. To this day those estates are producing rentals,—rentals far exceeding in value what they were producing in his day, and this, year by year, now for a century and a half; but in what other way than by the labours of four or five generations—the labour of ploughing, reaping, sowing, mowing, thatching, digging, and the thousand occupations of the farm? It is by the honest, ill-rewarded, and despised Guy's Hospital.

Labour produces rent. labours of the agricultural labourers that this rental swells the income of one heir succeeding another. Such considerations as these might prompt the owners of estates and other investments, the rather to look upon themselves as trustees, as responsible for the careful and judicious administration of their affairs, and restrain them from the absurd and lavish expenditures we so often see.

A new epoch. Obviously, society has arrived at an historical and new epoch, one of those periods out of which grow new departures from old institutions and usages, emancipations from ancient servitudes, and enfranchisement in long-deferred rights, or relapse into greater dependence and helplessness.

Comfort must be derived from the reflection that finance and its instrument, money, are, and will be, subjected to the laws of evolution. As surely as mankind have progressed from the merely physical or savage state to the physical intellectual (our present state), so surely will they advance to the moral, when the rule of unreasoning and self-defeating selfishness, of fraud and violence will cease. The great agent to forward this progressive march **Machinery the hand-maid of civilization.** of events is MACHINERY. This profitable, beneficial, and wealth-creating power, so far, has been the servant of the plutocratic and aristocratic classes, who have diverted what was meant for the general good, as the annihilator **Devices of the monied power.** of drudgery and excessive toil, to their own advantage, by combination, by confusing the councils of the producers, the workers, by inserting adroit clauses into important acts, to secure benefits surreptitiously, and, in America, by caucuses and rings, by control and ownership of the newspaper press, by the sophistries of professors of political economy, by the free use of money, by intimidation, by the suppression of discussion, by the perversion of literature, by the connivance of reporters in garbling speeches, and at last, in the final contest, would not hesitate by hiring mobs to intimidate opponents. " But the stars in their courses fight against Sisera." Rapid intercommunication of nations, printing, and above all, machinery, compel change and urge advance. Not a stroke of the steam-engine but quickens and necessitates social, political, and international, and above all, financial changes.

Machinery demands a monetary reform.

An American writer thus eloquently pictures the wonders effected by this gift of ingenuity to production :—

" Less than fifty years ago, civilization began a new era, in its wonderful development of steam, in the arts, and in locomotion. In that time it has more than quadrupled the producing capacity of the world. While on the one side steam has stimulated an enormous production, surpassing the anticipation of any in all former ages, on the other, it is taxing man's faculties to the utmost to create and devise new wants, in order to dispose of these commodities. So accustomed have we become to observe the various daily new applications of labour-saving discoveries, that we cease to be startled with their economy, nor do we any longer pause to estimate the enormous increase to production which they occasion. These great developments,

Machinery: its wonders.

however, are evidently in entire harmony with great organic laws, intended to force a higher civilization upon mankind, and [any new device to cheapen and enlarge the use of products, is surely working to that grand accomplishment, and is well worthy of your highest encouragement.*

Has encouraged usury.

At the dawning of this new era of discovery man still held to his old-fashioned ideas of high interest and usury, with which he at first emerged from barbarism. At each new invention of steam, electricity, chemistry, and general discovery, to be made subservient to his use and comfort, he called for larger issues of money. The capital of the world,

Requires an expansive money.

not unmindful of this sudden and unexpected tax upon its resources, through such large and rapid development, by inventing various devices of banking and monopoly of credit, seized upon the currency of the people to distribute it with high usury to producers. The money power has gone still farther. In its aim to secure large profits, it has usurped the power to contract and expand both the credit and the circulating medium of the people at its interest or pleasure, and the exercise of this unjustly-assumed prerogative has been the frightful source of panics and distress, by forcing industry to pay higher interest, rents, and profits than it can fairly earn. With the increasing necessity of the people for steam highways the money power saw still larger opportunities.

Machinery compels monetary reform.

"It pushed its shrewdly-contrived system of banking at extortionate interest rates on railroad securities, until

* For Rev. E. Palmer's denunciation of Usury, see App. T.

to-day the rail-highways of the world, chartered for public benefits, are doubled up and mortgaged to capital, at such rates as to compel producers to pay heavy fines for travelling on these railways which the producers themselves have made. Whether we will or not, this vast and rapid increase of commodities must be accepted as necessities, and be more largely utilized for the benefit of the whole people. We cannot if we would, put out the fires of labour-saving machinery, and set the sun of civilization backward. There is an irresistible force which is pushing us forward. There is no middle course. This inherent energy is demanding from you an encouragement to the industry of the people, that they may, one and all, produce commodities in a larger ratio than ever before; so that they may, one and all, consume more generously in the interest of advancing civilisation. Nor need you fear an over-production of diversified industries, for the people may safely be trusted to produce no more than they have the power of profitably consuming. Their general intelligence and industry may always be safely relied upon, as a true balance and regulator for production. What is the condition? On one side is the power of steam, by which man has suddenly developed an enormous power to produce. He has invented steamships, and steam-roads to carry these products to all parts of the country, and the world. Men need all these products,—all these commodities with all their prospective increase.

"They ask for the boon of earning, that they may be able

Money to increase with production.

to buy them. And to do this, they only ask of you that the volume of money may always and at all times keep pace with the volume of products. They ask that, as industry needs it, you will supply a sufficiency, and not, as hitherto, restrict it; that labour shall not be the prey of usurers and non-producers." *

Mr. Kellog on machinery.

Mr. Kellog has shown in his excellent work, "A New Monetary System," how the benefits which ought to have been derived from this wonder-working servant of man, have been neutralised, and even counteracted, by a barbarous metallic money.

Machinery requires an expansion of money.

"The labour-saving machines that have been invented within the last half century, have greatly facilitated production. Improvements in implements of husbandry have materially lessened agricultural labour; and most articles manufactured by machinery are made with less than one-fourth of the labour that was formerly required. We should naturally suppose that these improvements would be a great relief and advantage to the labouring classes; and that they would feel grateful to those who have studied out the laws of nature and invented the machines. Yet both the inventors of machinery, and the operatives in general, continue to toil on in want, and many of them have neither means nor leisure to educate their children. Increased facility in production seems to increase the number and multiply the wants of those who live in idle luxury, instead of affording

---

* F. B. Thurber, of New York: for his "Steam and Electricity," a valuable article contributed to the *International Review*, App. U.

the desired relief to actual producers. Fifty years ago, the farmers raised, carded, and spun their wool; they raised flax, and spun most of their linen; and cotton was also mostly carded and spun by each family to supply its own wants. Now, farmers who raise wool, cotton, and flax, sell the raw materials, which often pass through a number of hands before they reach the manufacturer. The manufactured goods again pass through several hands before they reach the consumer. Machinery has collected the people into towns and villages to work in large factories, where they sell their labour, and buy their board and clothing. This greatly augments the necessity for the exchange of goods, —the more machinery the greater the necessity for exchanges of products—yet there has been no new invention in financial affairs, by which the exchange may be more equitably and easily made. True, we have increased the amount of gold and silver coins, and the number of banks, bank-notes, and money brokers, but this is no more an improvement in the medium of distribution, than an increase in the number of pack-horses on the old muddy roads would be an improvement in conveying products.

"Just monetary laws are of more importance to the labouring classes than all the machinery that has been invented for the last fifty years. Let money expand with the wonderful expansion of production, and the producing classes, who will gain the benefit of all improvements, will rejoice at every advance in machinery, and the inventors will be hailed as the benefactors of mankind."—*Kellog's "New Monetary System."*

The working class, the nation.   This phrase "the working classes," that trips so glibly off the tongues of political economists and the propertied classes, is wrongly applied to men who live by labour. Labour, the great creator of all things, is enjoined as a duty and a· necessity upon the great majority of living men. Therefore they are the nation, and *"class"* applied to them is a misnomer.

Gold money an impediment to progress.   The *"auri sacra fames"* has afflicted the nations for ages, but the time is coming, be it in the next generation or the succeeding, when they will see through the great delusion.

The time will undoubtedly arrive when this scramble by great nations for the temporary possession of a few millions of gold will be remembered by statesmen with feelings of amused contempt for the financial ignorance of our age. The contentions of children for straws and feathers are not more frivolous.

Possessing, as Great Britain and America do, to which Canada may be added,* all the elements of national greatness—and that greatest of all, an industrious, thoughtful, and energetic population—there is no reason why the least impediment should be imposed to their growing prosperity by their monetary systems. A good system of money would greatly facilitate and advance the progress of the

* See William Brown's "Thoughts on Paper," and "Lending on Interest." Montreal, 1872. App. V.

two nations, while the present absurd and anomalous one is constantly retarding and checking it.

Under such a system labour would assert its dignity, and no longer be wasted on the dilettanti and fantastic tastes of the wealthy. The waste of labour on Mosaics in Florence is humorously described by Mark Twain. *Mark Twain on Mosaics. App. W.*

Let no nation think itself great as long as the condition of the great masses of the people is one of frequent depression, suffering, and poverty. A nation is truly great when the working classes, enjoying the blessings of free institutions, possess also their just proportion of the necessaries and comforts of life, which are the produce of their own toil and skill, and that with as little change or uncertainty of tenure as is compatible with the vicissitude of all human affairs.

We see no reason why the national debt should not be gradually but certainly liquidated, had we a representative paper money system. We see no reason why, with such a system, the money power should not be restrained within due limit, and the just claims of capital and labour adjusted. Under such a system, it is true that the vicious, the improvident, and the idle would still reap as they sow ; but every industrious, well-conducted, and intelligent Englishman and American would be in a greatly-improved condition. The greatest happiness of the greatest number would be effectually secured—and that is all that the wisest statesman can do. *Paper money would pay off national debt.*

Finally, and as a last word to the advocates of gold.

Your fear of over-issue, with the example of the assignats before us, is very natural, and easily accounted for;

But Paper Money must be the Money of the Future.

The proposal of the Liverpool Currency Reform Association is respectfully submitted to your candid consideration, namely, that the fundholder should, when there was a demand for money, have liberty to present his stock for conversion into legal-tender notes, resigning his annuity of 3½ per cent. On the contrary, when there was no demand for money, and it was too plentiful, he, on paying in his legal-tender notes, should, on their being cancelled, receive consols, and appear again as a creditor on the nation, and a recipient of his quota of the taxes.

This, as a temporary expedient, tending to keep the rate of discount or the price of money at 3½ per cent.

Any safeguards you propose will be discussed, and adopted if reasonable.

But no commodity—though of all commodities gold is the best—can fulfil the functions of a legal tender for all other commodities.

Metallic Money is Barter Disguised.

The discussion of Gold as against Paper is futile, and must give place to the discussion, PAPER MONEY—HOW TO BE ISSUED.

APPENDIX A.

NEWSPAPERS THE ORGANS OF CAPITALISTS.

ADMIRAL MAXSE has clearly shown that the newspaper press, so far from being the best possible instructor of the people, as Lord Brougham taught, is the mere organ of a leisured and dilettante class. "So far from the daily newspapers being the organs of thought, I have no hesitation in saying that they are organs for the *suppression* of much of the most earnest and vital thought in the country. They exist upon a false pretence. It seems to be generally ignored that they are founded purely upon a commercial basis ; their primary object being to sell as many copies as possible. They look to circulation among the paying class, and Radicalism is mostly an offence to the paying class. For this reason the *Morning Star* expired, and for the same reason successful journals are negative in thought; and though they assume extravagant pretensions to represent public opinion, they are the mere organs of wealth and trade. I do not blame them for this ; I am only anxious to expose the Radical misconception which treats them as veritable exponents of national thought. It may be easily shown that the main function of all the daily newspapers, commencing with the *Times* and ending with the *Echo*, is to cater to the amusement of a prosperous and dilettante public. The space and importance which have been daily accorded to gossip, intrigue, and exposure of private affairs, give us a useful measure of the character of the ordinary newspaper reader's demand. We are thus informed what is the most paying of newspaper ware. But there are certain standing features in the daily sheet which are apparently indispensable to its success. Who has ever known a daily paper, however great its press of Parliamentary debate or political speech, sacrifice its columns of ' Sporting Intelligence'? or, when do we miss the Stock and Share list ? How often do we find three columns of the *Times* devoted to an account of a drawing-room, or of the people who figure at a State Ball, or to the childish details of a royal procession ?

"It may seem to some that the obvious remedy for the unfairness and class character of existing daily journalism is to start a daily Radical organ. But a daily organ is the product of wealth and leisure ; and the class which is without representation in the daily press, although the most numerous, is without wealth and without leisure. Some £60,000 or £70,000 are necessary to start a London daily paper. Then, to ensure its success, a large daily subscription must be secured, and a heavy contribution by means of advertisements. These three requisites are entirely wanting. Where is the capital to come from in the first instance ? Secondly, working men cannot afford to pay sixpence a week for a newspaper, and genuine Radicals, in the paying class, find themselves in too sad a minority to be able to furnish the necessary contingent of readers. Finally, the advertisement fund would be entirely wanting, as advertisements, especially the most paying ones, are exclusively addressed to capitalists with money to invest. Is it likely that even if working men could afford to subscribe six-pence a week, many of them would be found with spare cash to invest in a Peruvian gold mine, or in schemes for irrigating the plains of Madras, or supplying water to towns in the Argentine republic ? "—" *Social Revolt.*" *By Captain Maxse.*

How the newspaper press treats the working men and their interests is thus shown by Admiral Maxse. Mr. Bradlaugh is the most influential of all their leaders of the present day, but his eloquent and powerful addresses are either suppressed or dis-missed in a paragraph.

"I myself was present at two of the largest meetings that have ever been held in London, where the working men were met to formulate their demands—the one at St. James's and the other at Exeter Hall. There was no Minister present at either of them to ascertain the wishes of the class whom the approaching legislation was intended to affect. The only means of their communication lay through the daily press : and the daily press hardly vouchsafed to notice them. I remember hearing at the same critical period, that Mr. Mill was going to make a speech on the Education ques-tion at the Society of Arts Room, and turning with eagerness on the following day to the daily newspaper for a report of his words, I looked in vain. There was in one or two papers a brief refer-ence to his appearance, with a scanty abridgment of his remarks, but the principal journals were too much engaged in spreading their usual saleable wares of sporting and stock-jobbing news, their theatrical and foreign gossip, University boat race odds, Hurlingham pigeon match handicaps, sensational divorce cases, and the last domestic grievance, to spare even a corner for the words of England's greatest political thinker upon a question respecting the fate of some two million neglected and helpless children."

It is a common error of political economists to identify the capitalist with the monied man. The one, the hard-working head of a large concern, an organiser of labour, and who may be termed a captain in the army of industry,—him they confound with the sleeping partner—the monied man, who sits quietly by and absorbs a share of the profits as interest of money. In fact, it may be doubted whether the persistent teachings of the political econo-mists, and the continuous efforts of the *Times, Telegraph,* and *Economist,* and also of monied men in general, to confound money and capital be the result of ignorance or design.

APPENDIX B.

DESCRIPTION OF THE STATE OF THE FACTORY TOWNS.

"A FEW steps out of the market-place or principal thorough-fare, you find yourself among long, straight, narrow streets, crossed, chiefly at right angles, by streets longer and narrower. Perhaps there is, or has been, a pavement of brick for the foot-passengers. By the time you have walked a few hundred yards the road is hardly levelled, much less gravelled; the irregularities of the surface forbid the supposition of sewers—in fact, you see no signs of them; you walk on cinders or "slag." Whole rows of habitations are built back to back, without any thorough ventilation, and with all the conveniences, dunghills, and dirt between the cot-tage door and the public road. There is no arrangement even to carry off the superficial water. There are rotten and dirty tubs to catch the rain water; and happy are they who find themselves within reasonable distance of a pump or a pond. The houses—that is, whole streets and suburbs—have been built by speculators, who have studied every art for the economy of space, material, and labour. If they can save a foot, if they can make half a brick do duty for a whole brick, and if they can cheat either the tenant, or the waywarden, or the collector, they know how to do so, and they will do it. As you advance, and get into what ought to be the country, you find growing laystalls and deepening quagmires. The brook which flows or stagnates by your side is black, or brown, or yellow, or blue, or mantling with various metallic hues, or altogether solid. Every here and there an irregular jetty of all kinds of rubbish thrown down the bank checks or turns the stream. The roads are very deep in mud or indescribable slime. What strikes you most is the utter absence of grace or pleasantness in everything around you, above or below. The atmosphere, of course, is thick; the pave-ment at the best is ashes or asphalte—probably much worse; every kind of nuisance is tolerated and undisturbed; the only idea of beauty is the endless straight line, though no attempt seems ever made to level the road or to make a uniform incline, even where it

Disgrace-ful state of the factory towns.

might be done very easily. The great want is water. The brooks come from the neighbouring moor, sometimes with excessive impetuosity and abundance; but no attempt has been made to collect and husband the supply at head-quarters. There are old tramroads and new railways, and even canals, all about, but no pure water, though within a few miles there are thousands of acres of moss and bog that only want tapping and draining. Should you have the opportunity of asking how it is that a population so prosperous has done so little for health and elegance, the answer is that their prosperity is the very reason for this want. The people are too busy, labour is too precious, life too short, for anything but money-getting. Everybody who has time or money is making his fortune, and cannot attend to the improvement of the neighbourhood. There are no country gentlemen to want good roads: there are no fine ladies to turn up their noses at nuisances. The people are at the mills all day; and as nothing ever comes into their streets except the coal cart or the cabbage truck, they do not want much paving. It is not their affair. They want amusement, they want drink, but they do not want fine streets, good roads, sewers, and pure water. They do not care much for public gardens, though there is hardly a man of them who would not like a little garden of his own, and who will not rent one if he can."—*Times.*

APPENDIX C.

Mr. Cobden's Evidence on the Evil Effects of Fluctuation on Business.

The evil effects of fluctuations—and it is the rate of discount varying that causes this fluctuation—were never explained in a more practical and impressive manner than was done by Mr. Cobden, before the Parliamentary Committee on Banks of Issue, in 1840. This was his statement:—

"I could adduce a fact derived from my own experience that would illustrate the heavy losses to which manufacturers were exposed in their operations by those fluctuations (in 1837) in the value of money.

"I am a calico printer; I purchase the cloth, which is my raw material, in the market; and have usually in warehouse three or four months' supply of material. I must necessarily proceed in my operations, whatever change there may be—whether a rise or fall in the market. I employ 600 hands, and those hands must be employed. I have fixed machinery and capital, which must also be kept going; and therefore, whatever the prospect of a rise or fall in prices may be, I am constantly obliged to be purchasing the material, and contracting for the material on which I operate. In 1837 I lost by my stock in hand £20,000, as compared with the stock-taking in 1835, 1836, and 1838; the average of those three years, when compared with 1837, shows that I lost £20,000 by my business in 1837; and what I wish to add is, that the whole of this loss arose from the depreciation in the value of my stock.

"My business was as prosperous; we stood as high as printers as we did previously; our business since that has been good, and there was no other cause for the losses I then sustained but the depreciation of the value of the articles in warehouse in my hands. What I wish particularly to show is, the defenceless condition in which we manufacturers are placed, and how completely we are at the mercy of these unnatural fluctuations. Although I was aware that the losses were coming, it was impossible that I could do otherwise than proceed onward—with the certainty of suffering a loss on the stock; to stop the work of 600 hands, and to fail to supply our customers, would have been altogether ruinous; that is a fact drawn from my own experience."

APPENDIX D.

MEMORIAL OF THE MERCHANTS OF LIVERPOOL TO LORD JOHN RUSSELL IN THE PANIC OF 1847.

THE following Memorial of the Merchants, etc., of Liverpool, sent up in all haste to Lord John Russell, then First Lord of Her Majesty's Treasury, during the panic of 1847, describes vividly the distress inflicted by the Bill of 1844. The merchants deemed it "needless on that occasion to inquire into the causes," and have ever since been equally quiescent.

"SHOWETH,—That your Memorialists beg respectfully to represent to your Lordship the present deplorable condition of the trade, commerce, and manufactures of the country, and the imperative necessity for such immediate relief as it may be in the power of Government to afford. Produce of every description is only saleable in small quantities and at an enormous sacrifice. Bills of exchange and the most valuable securities are inconvertible into cash even at great depreciation, except in most insignificant amounts. Foreign orders for produce and goods cannot be executed for want of the customary facilities for the disposal of bills drawn against them. Confidence is all but annihilated; and the currency of the country is in a great measure withdrawn and hoarded.

"*It is needless on this occasion to inquire by what combination of causes* this lamentable state of affairs has been brought about. A crisis of unparalleled severity exists, and your Memorialists believe that it is in the power of Government to allay alarm and restore confidence by coming to the relief of the commercial and manufacturing classes, *by a temporary advance on the credit of the country.*

"Your Memorialists believe that it is not only the interest but the duty of Government to afford relief, insomuch as they confidently believe that the utter prostration of the manufacturing and commercial interests cannot otherwise be prevented, whereby the labouring population will be immediately thrown out of employment, and an amount of misery and destitution witnessed unexampled in the history of the country.

"Your Lordship may depend upon us when we assure you that if the present pressure be not removed, merchants and other traders of undoubted respectability, who are not only solvent, but rich, and have merchandise and bills which, under ordinary circumstances, would afford ample means of meeting engagements, will inevitably be compelled to stop payment."

Another experience of Liverpool as to the benefits of advances was afforded by the Common Council of that town in the year 1793 :—

A panic relatively as great as that of 1847, devastated the trade of that port, with all the symptoms as indicated above. The Council applied to Parliament for powers to issue Corporation Notes based on the credit of the Corporation estate. Though empowered to issue £500,000, they found a much smaller amount sufficient to "stay the plague." Business revived, and everything resumed its usual aspect of cheerful activity.

⸴ APPENDIX E.

FALL IN THE PRICE OF CORN CAUSED BY THE RETURN TO CASH PAYMENTS.

THE following was a statement furnished by Lord John Russell, in 1842, of the price of wheat under Mr. Pitt's inconvertible notes, and under Sir Robert Peel's Act, making the sovereign our only money :—

In 1816 the price was	78s.	per quarter.	
1817	,,	...... 96s.	,,
1818	,,	...... 86s.	,,
1819	,,	..... 74s.	,,
1820	,,	...... 67s.	,,

After the return to cash payments :—

In 1821 the price was ...... 56s. per quarter
1822   „   ..... 44s.   „
1823   „   ...... 52s.   „
1824   „   ...... 63s.   „
1825   „   ...... 68s.   „

The effects of such a revolution in prices inflicted greater evils than a foreign invasion. The farmers, as a body, were ruined. They emigrated in numbers to America, and some who had made a comfortable living under the war prices, as they were called, were seen breaking stones on the high-road.

Mr. Ricardo, a great authority, and who strongly advocated the change, declared, with the whole of the bullionist party, that prices would only fall to the extent of 5 per cent. He, however, lived to change his opinion, and shortly before he died, confessed that he had done so.*

APPENDIX F.

NATIONAL DEBTS.†

WITHOUT going into the question of the justice' of exacting gold interest on a paper debt, it may be well to look into the way in which the debt has been contracted, and to see whether the sums debited to the nation have really been contracted.

The plan adopted of making the capital vary in amount, instead of the rate of interest varying, is a source of complication which adds to the difficulties of finance. In addition to this, the plan adopted of creating stock, *i.e.*, debt, beyond the gold received, opened a door to a deception and fraud little understood.

" Sir John Sinclair states that between the years 1776 and 1786 (this date is taken because previous to 1776 the debt was so small as compared with what it was afterwards, that it need not be taken into account), stock was created to the extent of 115 millions, whilst the cash received was only 92 millions. Plainly interpreted this means, that whilst the nation only received 92 millions in gold, it was debited on the national ledger with 115 millions, and on that 115 millions engaged to pay interest. Mr.

---

* The late Sir William Heygate was with him when he made this confession. "Aye, Heygate, you and a few others who opposed us on cash payments have proved right. I said that the difference at most would only be 5 per cent., and you said that at the least it would be 25 per cent." This anecdote is given on the authority of the late Jonathan Duncan.

† "The National Debt Financially Considered : " a Prize Essay for the Society of Arts. By Edward Capps.

Capps had already, as a sample of the mode in which money was raised at this period, given the particulars of the loan of 1781, by which 21 millions of stock, or paper debt, was created for 12 millions cash received.

" We now come to the period of the French revolutionary war, which may be considered to have extended, with short intervals, from 1793 to the battle of Waterloo in 1815. It was during this period that the pernicious system of financing, which we have been describing, received its fullest development and reached its greatest proportions, the magnitude of the operations of this period so far transcending all previous transactions of the like nature as to make the latter sink into utter insignificance in the comparison. It would be tedious, and comparatively useless, to detail minutely the terms and circumstances of each loan. It will be sufficient to say, that, taking an average of all the loans, from the year 1793 to the year 1816, upwards of £173 of debt was created for every £100 money received. Marshall gives the following as the rate at which the loans were contracted in each year :—

YEAR	Money received. £	* Stock created for every £100 money. £
1793	100	140
1794	100	157
1795	100	163
1796	100	180
1797	100	215
1798	100	207
1799	100	177
1800	100	158
1801	100	174
1802	100	132
1803	100	173
1804	100	185
1805	100	177
1806	100	167
1807	100	159
1808	100	162
1809	100	161
1810	100	152
1811	100	166
1812	100	180
1813	100	184
1814	100	154
1815	100	191

being on an average, for the whole period, of £173 stock created for cash £100 money received."

It follows that the country only received 339 millions, instead of 586 millions, and that the additional 250 millions was thus saddled

* To the uninitiated it may be necessary to explain that the lender of every £100 had his name down in the national ledger as creditor for £140 or £191, as in 1815.

upon the country by its being artificially added to the capital of
the debt, by the mode of raising the money.

"The only loan," says Marshall, "created in 1816, was 8
millions from the Bank of England. That, with the surplus of the
loans raised in 1815, supplied the means of applying 18 millions
to the purchase of stock, at an average rate of £62 for 3 per
cent. stock; while in the preceding year, 62 millions of 3 per cent.
loan, and 8½ millions of 4 per cent. stock were created for only 35
millions, not money received, being at the rate of little more than
£50 of money received for every £100 of 3 per cent. stock
created.

"Paying a price of £62 for an article and then only valuing it
at £50 when you pay it away, or in other words, contracting a
debt of £52 in order to discharge obligations to the amount of
£50 needs no comment."

Now what object is all this meant to serve? Only to make the
people who are taxed to pay the fundholder, (i.e., the man who
had money to spare) believe that they were paying only 3 per cent.
for the debt when the fact was they were paying 6 and 7 per
cent.

The funding system is little understood. Eliminating the money
element, it means that one generation, we will say, for the purposes
of defence, calls upon the wealthy portion, that is, on those who
have stores of food, clothing, and (in the case of armies) tents,
stores of iron for ordnance and rifles, stores of sulphur, nitre, and
charcoal, of timber for ships of war, to give forth of the supplies
they possessed, for the common defence, under a payment from the
taxes of so much gold; but the gold has to be got from those who
are in possession of the coveted metal. But the possessors, or
capitalists demand more than 3 per cent. for their treasures: they
have to be bribed with more liberal offers, but the nation is to be
hoodwinked, and made to believe that it is only paying 4 per cent.
Hence the difference between stock and money paid, as given in the
above table.

But how are these millions raised? Here comes in the stock
jobber, the loan contractor, and the high financier. He takes the
loan, nominally £100 stock, but he only undertakes to pay 70 or 80
guineas, or new sovereigns. He has not these millions, but he
goes into the Stock Exchange and advertises the loan in small
shares, which are taken up by all the propertied class who have
guineas or sovereigns in their strong box to invest. The loan
contractor washes his hands of the affair, and lies in wait for a new
loan.

The generation raising the loan thus throws the burthen on
future generations by the process of interest, and their children
and children's children find that they are mulcted for the wants of
their forefathers. Those who had to oppose the ambitious schemes

of a Louis the Fourteenth contrived by this cunning financial operation to throw the burthen on their grandchildren, who had to maintain a struggle for national existence against a Napoleon.

The interest already paid on the debt amounts to 8,000 millions. What will be paid by the time that we enter on another century ?

APPENDIX G.

JEWS AND ARMENIANS IN THE EAST.

THAT the influence of the Jews in the East is altogether evil is shown by the following extract from the *Times* of Feb. 5th, which, besides their well-known system of usury, accuses them of establishing spirit shops, demoralizing the natives by giving them crédit with interest, thus holding whole villages in their grasp :—

" The view taken by Dr. Sandwith as to the evil influence of the Jews settled in the villages of Eastern Europe is strongly confirmed by the well-known author, Charles Boner, in his valuable work on ' Transylvania,' published in 1865. At page 617 he says : —' A great evil attending the leasing of these spirit shops to Jews is the increased number of them who thus settle in every part of the country. Their presence might not, at first sight, seem to bear upon the question of spirit drinking, but it does ; it is in close connexion with it. " When a Jew settles in a village," said a Protestant clergyman to me one day, when speaking on this subject, " you may be quite sure that the demoralization of the population will soon follow." This opinion only confirmed what I had been told many years before regarding the Jews in Bohemia, and especially in Galicia : careful observers in those two Provinces had expressed the same opinion. There, too, the small publichouses are leased wholly by Jews. They give credit with interest for the gin the peasant has not the ready money to pay for, thus putting it always within his reach. Unable to resist temptation, he gets more and more involved, till at last the inexorable usurious creditor seizes on his goods, his cattle, and his estate. In the two Provinces named above, the Jew publican, or he at the huckster's shop, literally holds the whole village in his grasp. It is his interest that it should be so ; nor does he rest till this desired state of dependence has been brought about. He knows that once within his net there is no escape, and that each day makes the victim more surely his.' This testimony is most valuable as the author is known to have been an intelligent observer and a most trustworthy and impartial writer."

A striking instance of the power of usury to bring down an

empire to the depths of humiliation and to the verge of social dissolution is afforded by Turkey, on which the eyes of all Europe have been anxiously fixed for the last twelve months. Though other agencies for evil have doubtless been at work, yet the most powerful have been the exorbitant demands of Armenians, Greeks, Christians, and Jews for the use of money. The rapacity of Pashas, who are compelled by the uncertainty of their tenure of office to accumulate wealth quickly, must be acknowledged ; yet the statements of R. A. Arnold are entitled to consideration. Turkey, a byword for bad government, can trace much of her misery to the exactions of Christians and Jews ; for the Mohammedans themselves are debarred by law, by custom, and religion, from exercising a profession anathematized by their creed and discreditable in the eyes of society. That the Turkish Government has borrowed money and allowed itself to dabble in the funding system is true, but these speculators, who were tempted by the high interest offered by the Porte, must recollect that that high interest only showed that they were playing a dangerous game, forgetting the axiom of the Duke of Wellington, " that high interest was an index of risk " ; and they must also bear in mind that if they could secure 15 per cent. for seven years they had their principal back, and the question is whether the money lender should have more repaid him than what he advanced.

Mrs. Burton, in her interesting work " Inner life of Syria," lifts the curtain and describes the shameless and unconscionable doings of these financial vampires. Mr. Burton, as Consul at Damascus, did what lay in his power to control and repress their rapacity, but on garbled and interesting representations forwarded by this race, who in all ages have devoted all their abilities and their energies to finance and money lending, the interest of the Rothschilds, Montifiores, Goldschmids, Goschens, and others was secured. Mr. Burton was removed from the Consulship,—matters resumed their former aspect,—the inevitable consequences ensued. The population is assuming a dangerous and threatening attitude, and the last accounts from Damascus anticipate troubles and even massacres.

Mr. R. A. Arnold, in his recent work on the Levant, thus describes the relations subsisting between Christian and Turk :—

" The Armenian scale varies from 24 to 60 per cent., sometimes by express contract, sometimes as a disguised loan, frequently by compound interest. All classes are victims, but the chief sufferers are the poor, and more especially the peasant. No Turkish, no Arab landlord would dream of selling out or evicting a tenant, but our 'Eastern Christian' will ; and when, as is frequently the case, the usurer can gain to his help the strong arm of the Government, eviction, with all its results of cruel misery and violence—for Whiteboys are not peculiar to Ireland—is carried over wide tracts. Entire villages have been unroofed, and cultivated lands left to pasture or to downright desolation. The European traveller, primed with staple ideas about Turkish oppressions, the Sultan's horse-hoofs, barbarian rule, and the like, sees the ruin along the wayside, and notes for subsequent publication his observations on the decadence of the Turkish empire and the fatal results of Ottoman or Mohammedan rule,—observations which his Greek dragoman will sedulously confirm ; and these will, perhaps, be repeated and believed in Parliament. But could he know the active cause of all this desolation, his visionary Pasha tyrant would fade away, and would transform himself into no other than some wealthy money lender—the usurer—whose cent. per cent. has taken away ' the upper garment and the very millstone, not for pledge, but sale.' "

If there is any truth in the principles advocated, it follows that of the combatants, Turkey and Russia, now preparing for hostilities, whichever avails itself of a paper money issued by its government and which it will receive as quittance of taxation, will conquer the other,—should that other obstinately adhere to barbarous prejudice.

APPENDIX H.

The Money Question—Distress in America—Mr. William A. Berkey.*

I received a book (p.p. 880) from the author, Mr. William A. Berkey, of Grand Rapids, Michigan ; and which, with many others, have been addressed to me from America: these in return for sundry copies of Rector Twells's tracts and extracts from Bishop Berkely's "Querist." This pamphlet, by the late Reverend John Twells, is not so voluminous as the works from the other side ; but, being brief, lucid, and referring particularly to the financial history of the "United States, even back to the time when they were colonies, its circulation in a cheap stereotyped form has been recommended to the reformers there. The following is the description which Mr. Berkey gives of the present state of that once flourishing nation in his valuable contribution to the history of his country. He opens with drawing a contrast between the years 1865 and 1876 :—

"In 1865, when the rebellion terminated, the producing forces of the Northern and Western States,—the working men, the land, the machinery, the mines, the water power, etc.—were developing

* "The Money Question." By William A. Berkey, Grand Rapids, Michigan.

wealth in every possible direction, and the people, individually free from debt, were in the enjoyment of unparalleled prosperity. The wealth of the nation, in spite of the ravages of war, had increased as it had never done before. The assessed valuation of the property of the nation in 1870, notwithstanding the ruined condition of the South, was over $30,000,000,000, as against $16,000,000,000, in 1860. Out of the abundance of these productions the people were enabled to meet all the demands of the government with ease. The Federal Government, indeed, began to pay off the public debt rapidly. But in carrying out the policy of the monied power, it first paid off, by substituting bonds, all those forms of indebtedness of the government which served the purposes of money, thus depriving the producing forces of the nation of their most important tool.

"Now, the American people are poor and in debt. Nearly all forms of productive industry are paralysed, and the channels of trade are stagnant or sluggish. Their estate is rapidly depreciating in value, which will inevitably result in a general foreclosure of mortgages and transfer of property from the debtor to the creditor class throughout the country. Instead of a million of non-producers carrying muskets, as was the case during the war, there are now several millions of people, who would gladly work for a mere subsistence, in a state of enforced idleness, living on the bitter bread of public or private charity. The nation is scarcely producing more than the necessities of life, and yet the people are told that the present condition of affairs is due to over-production and the like causes. The only over-production troubling the nation just now is an over-production of rascals and fools— rascals who teach such nonsense to divert the public mind from the true source of the trouble, and the fools who believe it. Since the attempt to re-establish a false monetary system by means of contraction has worked such wide-spread ruin, it would seem but the part of common wisdom for the people to demand a different policy, if not from conviction at least as an experiment. It certainly could not make matters worse."

*   *   *   *   *   *   *

- "It is high time that everybody should seek to understand this question, because, until the national banks are destroyed and a system of money is founded upon sound principles, there can be no enduring prosperity in the country, and the independence of the people will be a mere phantom. The demoralization which is now going on throughout the country in consequence of the enforced idleness and poverty of millions of people is a matter of serious import, and one which should awaken to a sense of duty and action every Christian man and woman in the land, and especially ministers of the Gospel, who profess to follow Him whose tenderest care was ever manifested for the weak, the lowly, and the oppressed."

Mr. Berkey tells us that this vampire class not only call to their aid a subservient body of writers, and an unscrupulous and scurrilous newspaper press, but are prepared, if their threats and denunciations are to be believed, to resort to extreme measures. He gives another fact, "which may convey a warning to those who are lending themselves to the ignoble cause of enriching the monied power at the expense of ruin, distress, and poverty to the masses. When the American people are driven to the extremity that the English and Scotch people were by an attempt to force resumption, and when they gather in vast multitudes, as the English did at Peterloo, and the Scotch at Glasgow, to demand redress, matters will assume a very different shape in the United States from what they did in Great Britain. It is true that an *organ of a notorious Wall Street operator, the 'New York Tribune' has intimated that any such demonstrations would promptly be met with ' shot and slaughter,'* but in the United States that is more easily said than done. The day has not yet arrived when Americans can be intimidated by such threats.

"As yet, 'they their duties know, but know their RIGHTS, and knowing, dare maintain them!' While the American people undoubtedly possess too much patriotism and intelligence to jeopardize the stability of their institutions, they nevertheless may possibly forget in the hour of their distress that the Lord hath said ' Vengeance is mine.'

" In that day the Shermans and MacCullochs had better never have been born ! "—The threat of the *Tribune* is similar in spirit to the Duke of Wellington's, "If the people are not quiet there is a way to make them."

Bitter recrimination, ever-growing exasperation, heated controversies indicate earnest and intensified feeling, and seem to forebode a troubled future for that once happy country. How different from the stupor and apathy which prevail here. This stolid indifference to this vital question is owing to the literature and the newspapers of the day being under the influence of the monied power. That wonderful production, "that matutinal wonder," the *Times*, is their professed and acknowledged organ, and its influence over the provincial press is supreme, whilst, as Bonamy Price truly says, " the advocacy of paper money has disappeared from English literature, and no writer of acknowledged authority can be found to defend it." One exception he might have made ;—John Ruskin, whose influence is great and increasing, is forming a school of thought and a band of disciples who will very soon make themselves felt.

Mr. Berkey quotes the following extract from a report of a legislative Committee of the State of New York, so early as 1818 :—

" ' Of all aristocracies none more completely enslaves a people than that of money; and in the opinion of your Committee, no system was ever devised so perfectly to enslave a community as that of the present mode of conducting banking establishments. Like the siren of the fable, they entice to destroy. They hold the purse strings of society, and, by monopolizing the whole of the circulating medium of the country, they form a precarious standard, by which all the property of the country,—houses, lands, debts, and credits, personal and real estate of all descriptions—are valued, thus rendering the whole community dependent upon them ;—proscribing every man who dares to expose their unlawful practices. If he happens to be out of their reach, so as to require no favours from them, his friends are made the victims. So no one dares complain.

" ' The Committee, on taking a general view of our State, and comparing those parts where banks have been for some time established with those which have none, are astonished at the alarming disparity. They see, in the one case, the desolation they have made in societies that were before prosperous and happy; the ruin they have brought on an immense number of the more wealthy farmers, and they and their families suddenly hurled from wealth and independence into the abyss of ruin and despair. If the facts stated in the foregoing be true, (and your Committee have no doubt they are) together with others equally reprehensible and to be dreaded, their influence will too frequently, nay, often already begins to assume a species of dictation altogether alarming, and unless some judicious remedy is ' provided by legislative wisdom, we shall soon witness attempts to control all elections to offices in our counties, nay, the elections to the very legislative Senators and members of assembly, will be indebted to the banks for their seat in the capital, and thus the wise end of our civil institutions will be prostrated in the dust by corporations of their own raising.'— p. 127.

*　　*　　*　　*　　*　　*　　*

"In a state of civilization, money performs an important part in the production, distribution, and accumulation of wealth; it is necessary therefore that it should be based on sound principles. A great deal of nonsense has been written about money and its hidden power, partly through ignorance, and partly through design. So widely have political economists differed in regard to its nature and functions, that it is not surprising that people have been willing to ascribe to it some mysterious power, or that they should have almost despaired of being able to comprehend the principles on which it is founded, and by which its movements are governed. And this delusion has been encouraged in every way possible by the monied and governing classes, who are thus enabled to found systems of money on the false theory that money is the master and not the servant of labour and property.

"But the age is characterized by a spirit of progress, and old systems are rapidly yielding to new ones. The signs of the times indicate that the hoary tyranny of the money power, which has exercised despotic sway for ages over the masses of mankind, will sooner or later be compelled to succumb to the influences of an enlightened public sentiment. A distinguished English writer, Sir John Barnard Ryles, in commenting on the imperfect and rudimentary condition of the science of political economy, says : ' The steam engine, steam navigation, mechanical inventions, the electric telegraph, modern chemistry have not appeared for nothing. A science of political economy will yet dawn, that shall perform as well as promise,—a science that will rain the riches of nature into the laps of the starving poor. MEN DO NOT YET DREAM OF THE PROSPERITY WHICH IS IN STORE FOR ALL ORDERS OF THE PEOPLE.'

"A large and increasing number of leading thinkers, statesmen, and philanthropists of the day are calling public attention to the unequal and unjust distribution of the products of industry that is constantly going on, through the agency of a false and corrupt monetary system, and their views have already made a profound impression on the public mind. The ignorant masses of Great Britain may be deluded into believing—as is taught by the dismal school of English political economists—that it is natural, and if natural proper—though we may not see the reason—that poverty, and want, and disease, and misery, should be the next-door neighbour of wealth and unbounded prosperity ; but the intelligent farmers, mechanics, and labourers of the United States are not so easily convinced that the surplus wealth, which their labour produces annually, should naturally be owned at the end of the year by the financiering and non-producing classes of the country. When people find themselves being robbed, they are apt to try to discover the offender and the means by which it is accomplished. A very moderate amount of investigation, we think, will satisfy any candid mind that the theory, that the money power is the robber which deprives labour of its just reward, and that a corrupt money system is the instrumentality by means of which the robbery is perpetuated, is based on sound reasons."—*Berkey*, p. 25.

APPENDIX I.

LIST OF PERSONS WHO HAVE DIED, LEAVING FORTUNES EXCEEDING
A QUARTER OF A MILLION.

(From the " Illustrated London Almanac.")

From 1863 to 1876.

1863.

E. Lloyd, Combe House, Croydon	...£600,000
S. D. Smith, Taumb Park	... 500,000

1864.

H. Huth, Harley-st.	...£500,000
The Duke of Cleveland	... 800,000
Sir R. P. Glyn	... 500,000
The Rev. J. Arkwright, Essex	... 400,000
Sir W. Brown, Liverpool	... 900,000
John Hayne, Hyde Park	... 400.000
H. Gurney, Norfolk	...1,000,000

1865.

J. Bates, Boston, U.S.	...£600,000
R. Burrow, Derbyshire	... 500,000
The Duke of Northumberland	... 500,000
The Marchioness of Londonderry	... 400,000
Richard Thornton	...2,800,000
·Pantia Ralli, Connaught-pl.	... 400,000
F. Williams, Worcester	... 400,000
Sir B. Heywood	... 400,000

1866.

W. H. Lumbton, Chesham-pl.	...£500,000
F. D. Goldsmid	... 400,000
Don Pedro Gonzales de Candamo	800.000
J. Ashbury, Manchester	400.000
Peter Arkwright, Willersley	... 800,000
W. H. Goschen, London	... 500,000
T. A. Gibbs, Lancaster-gt	... 400,000

1867.

H. F. Mildmay, Sevenoaks	...£400,000
J. G. Abbott, Newcastle	... 600,000
W. A. Sparrow, Staffordshire	... 600,000
Alexander Cunningham	... 600,000

Charles Hardy, Kent	... £500,000
Hollingworth Maguire, Lombard-st.	... 600.000
W. Crawshay, Oxen	... 2,000,000
Lord Aveland	... 400,000
John Lewis, London and Paris	... 500,000

1868.

John Ames, Devon	... £500,000
Peter Pantia Ralli	... 500,000
Samuel Ayres, Leeds	... 1,200,000
H. Houldsworth, Glasgow	... 400,000
T. Bridges, Surrey	... 600,000
Sir B. L. Guinness, Dublin	... 1,100,000
The Earl of Northampton	... 700,000
E. Majoribanks	... 600,000

1869.

Don Christobel de Murietta	... £600,000
Joseph Crossley, Halifax	... 900,000
W. Cook; Kent	... 600,000
Sir C. Cunard	... 300,000
Samuel Scott, Cavendish-sq.	... 1,400,000
W. Stephenson Davidson	... 400,000
Robert Gosling, Fleet-st.	... 700,000
W. H. Foreman, Dorking	... 1,000,000
Mr. Peabody	... 400,000

1870.

The Marquis of Westminster	... £800,000
Don Gregorio de Meir y Feran	... 500,000
Thomas Fielden, Crumpsell	... 1,300,000
Thomas Parr, Hayes	... 500,000
W. T. West. Clapham Park	... 500,000
John Brocklehurst, Macclesfield	... 800,000
Miss E. Atherton, Kersell Cell	... 400,000
Thomas Thornton, Brixton	... 900,000

1871.

T. Brocklehurst, Macclesfield	... £600,000
Lord Hotham	... 500,000
The Right Hon. Lord H. Bentinck	... 500,000
B. Bacon Williams, Crown Court	... 500,000
Baron N. de Rothschild	... 1,800,000
Mrs. Augusta Ivers Mary Dixon	... 400,000
The Rev. J. Williams, Herts	... 500,000
The Marquis of Hertford	... 500,000
Giles Loader, Clarendon-pl.	... 3,000,000
J. A. T. Smith, Hyde Park	... 400,000

1872.

T. D. Castillo, Château de Condé	£600,000
James Lewis, Oldham	500,000
Lord Lonsdale	700,000
D. Cave, Gloucester	400,000
R. D. Bryne, Brabant Court	400 000
Sir F. Crossley	800,000
The Duke of Bedford	600,000
E. Walker, Lincoln's-Inn	500,000
Sir Charles Mills	700,000
Thomas Brassey	3,000,000
Mrs. Maria Maryon Brown	250,000
Thomas Dent, Hyde Park	500,000
Edward Harvey, Beddington	300,000

1873.

Laurence Levy, Westbourne Terrace	£300,000
Sir Thomas Beckett, Lincoln	350,000
Samuel Moses Samuel	500,000
John Hargarves, Accrington	400,000
Francis Wright, Derby	£700,000
Sir William Tite	1,000,000
Nathan Lees, Cheshire	400,000
Francis Toone, Hastings	400,000
Charles Pease, Darlington	350,000
Sir G. C. G. Wolverton	1,000,000
The Right Hon. Sir R. R. Westbury	300,000

1874.

W. Leaf, Streatham, Surrey	£300,000
The Earl of Egmont	350,000
Bryce Allan, Liverpool	250,000
Samuel Beale, Berks	350,000
August Gagnicre, London	400,000
John Wormald, Islington	250,000
Wm. Joynson, Kent	350,000

1875.

Roger Lyon Jones, Liverpool	£350,000
Wm. Tarn, Chislehurst	500,000
John Hargraves, Berks	600,000
Joseph Love, Durham	1,000,000
Struts, Derbyshire	900,000
Lady Vane	250,000
Joseph Goff	350,000
Virgil Pomfret	400,000
Henry Adderly	250,000
Mr. Wm Gibbs, Bristol	800,000

Charles Turner, M.P., Liverpool	...	...	...	£700,000
J. A. Arbuthnot, Windsor	...	...	...	400,000
Peter Ormrod, Lancashire	...	...	...	700,000
Robert Allfrey, Berkshire	...	...	...	400,000
James Houghton, Liverpool	...	...	...	250,000
Wynn Ellis, Whitstable ...	...	...	...	600,000
William P. Herrick	...	...	...	800,000
Rt. Hon. G. A. F. B. Howe	...	...	...	250,000
Rt. Hon. J. W. Hogg, Grosvenor Crescent	...	...	250,000
James Baird, Cambusoon	...	...	...	1,190,000
Earl of Sheffield ...	...	...	...	300,000
H. K. Belstone, Manchester	...	...	...	250,000
Charles Lambert, Upper Thames-st.	...	...	...	900,000

1876.

Henry Moses, Regent's Park	...	...	...	£600,000
William Graham, Clerkenwell ...	...	...	...	300,000
Sir W. Jackson, Birkenhead	...	...	...	700,000
Philip L. Hinds, Portland-place	...	...	...	250,000
Henry W. Nun, Isle of Wight ...	...	...	...	400,000
Marquis Cunyingham, Meath	...	...	...	500,000

Ten millions! This immense sum, by the machinery of rent and interest, is abstracted from the labour of mind and body of workers, aided by horse and steam power. It must be an effective industry that can raise such immense sums.

APPENDIX J.

Mr. Justice Byles—"Usury Laws Defended—By their Repeal Usury no longer Penal."

A small book on the subject was published in England, in 1845, by Mr. Justice Byles, then serjeant-at-law, containing practical opinions regarding legal restraints on lending on interest. These practical views are of great importance and are embodied in the following extracts:—

"But our own courts of common law, bankruptcy courts, and courts for the relief of insolvent debtors, present daily instances of cruel extortion, in comparison of which the instances afforded by the evidence given before the Lords' Committee (of 1841) and Lord Devon's Committee, are mildness and mercy. A loan at the rate of sixty per cent. per annum is not considered at all extortionate by those who have the means of knowing what takes place between distressed tradesmen, or gambling speculators, and money lenders or discounters of bills. A loan of £80, for which a promissory note or bill for £100 at a month is given, would be

considered reasonable. But that is interest at the rate of 300 per
cent. per annum. Whenever an impartial Parliamentary Committee shall institute a searching inquiry in the proper quarter,
they will find that interest at 100, 200, 300, 500 per cent. per
annum, and more, is amongst vast multitudes paid, or promised to
be paid, for the use of money; they will find reckless speculation
promoted, borrowers ruined, and the resources of the country mis-
applied and wasted; they will find in every court of common law
the most cruel actions constantly brought to enforce these extortionate demands ; actions *in which the law, so far from being as she
ought to be, the handmaid of justice, is in reality prostituted, and
made an accomplice in the perpetration of the most iniquitous gambling
and robbery.*

"If it be asserted that these evils (those of the property of
creditors being lost by usurious interest paid by debtors) existed
before the change in the law, the only proper and true answer *is a
denial of the assertion.* They did not in any considerable degree.
Here and there an instance might be found of a successful evasion
of the old law, but such instances were comparatively rare.
*Usurious interest was the exception, but now it is fast becoming the
rule.*

"The power to lend money at a high rate of interest secured by
law presents an easy expedient for evading the legal responsibilities
of partnership, which when generally understood by persons of large
fortune, will be often resorted to; enabling them to participate
largely in the profits of trade without sharing its losses, or without
rendering their property liable to the creditors of the concern.

"'Qui sentit commodum,' says the law, 'sentire debit et onus.'
If you really participate in the profits, or even lead the public to
believe you do, you, with your whole estate, shall be liable for the
losses."

In answer to the statement often put forth in defence of the
money-lending system, that people are the best judges of their own
interest, Justice Byles brings forward many instances to the contrary. "For example, the Acts of Parliament regulating annuity
contracts for the benefit of the grantor—the prohibition of the
truck system, or compelling to pay in the coin of the realm—the
compulsion to put important contracts in written form, and for the
parties to sign their names to them—the compulsion, in other
cases, to have a professional man present to explain the effects of
a warrant of attorney or cognovit etc.,—the prevention of the sale
of unwholesome meat, not leaving it to the mere buyers and sellers
—the power the law gives of entering shops and stalls to examine
weights and measures, thus actively interfering to prevent buyers
being cheated—the assay mark on gold and silver plate which
gives confidence and facility in dealing in these articles—the taxing
of attorneys' bills, by which a master of one of the courts looks

over the bill, and says how much the client ought to pay—the law
making it penal in hop-growers to pack their hops falsely—the laws
regulating steamboats and passage of emigrants—the factories' bills,
and regulations of mines, where the *adult* workman is protected
often by means which he would never have thought of—the compulsory education of professional men, doctors, and attorneys—the
laws against gaming and gaming policies on ships and lives—and
restraints on accumulations, by which trusts for that purpose beyond certain limits are prohibited. Let us even take the restraint
of the over issue of paper without security as a case in point, for
experience has demonstrated that no set of men can be entrusted
with such a power. To protect the simple, the ignorant, and the
necessitous, he justly adds, is not therefore an endless and hopeless
task.

"There is very little truth in the assertion that the usury laws
were inoperative because so often evaded. The words of the law
were large enough to meet every case. No matter how the
advance is made, in goods or in any other form, if the real contract
were a *loan*, the law looked through the outward form at the substance. 'Where the real truth is a loan of money,' said Lord
Mansfield, 'the wit of man cannot find a shift to evade the statute.'
There is no tribunal on earth for sifting facts and motives in commercial matters that will bear a moment's comparison with a
London special jury at Guildhall. Every cloak and disguise is
soon stripped off, and the truth stands naked before them. Nor
have juries hesitated to find the truth by their verdict, even when
it exposed the lender to the loss of his whole principal and to
imminent peril of the severest penalties besides.

"Advances of goods, apparent sales or re-sales of goods,
unusual and extravagant commissions on discounts or advances,
loans and pretended purchases of stock, and loans on continuation,
pretended wagers, pretended subleases, and a hundred other ingenious but futile devices of lenders, have been successively
defeated and branded as usurious; till at last it was discovered by
experience that no man could invent a way of lending money at
more than five per cent. interest, which would not be void in
law, and moreover highly penal."

He continues :—"Then it is urged, where people borrow in spite
of the law, the penalties which are incurred by the lender enhance
the risk. The value of that augmentation of the risk must be paid
by the borrower in the shape of yet higher interest, and so usury
laws injure the very persons whom they were designed to protect.

"But, in the first place, if there is any truth in the preceding
observations; if the old laws, generally speaking, regulated the
rate of interest, and the violations of the law were exceptions comparatively insignificant in number and amount, then, even were
this observation well-founded in practical truth, it would not be

deserving of much weight. For the case would then stand thus. Generally speaking, the usury laws succeed and are obeyed (see House of Commons' Committee, 1818, and of the Lords, 1841). The transactions in which they are violated are, both in number and amount, a minute fraction of those in which they are obeyed. Yet a superadded inconvenience, felt by this very small number of persons who violate the law, is put forward as a valid argument against the law altogether."

It appears by the testimony of witnesses before various parliamentary committees, that the general effect of the old law fixing five per cent. was to oblige the lender to content himself with the five per cent. when he could have got more.

In answer to the objection that legal limits cause the borrower to pay only the more heavily for his accommodation, experience shows that the borrower does not really pay for any enhanced legal risk caused by usury laws. Mr. Justice Byles says on this point : " Of late there has been, as to the majority of transactions, no penalties of usury. Has there been any alleviation of the extortionate usury, because the lender incurs no penalty ? On the contrary, we have seen, without any risk of penalties, interest extorted as monstrous as could have been done were the risk of penalties still existing. The enormous premiums extorted to cover the risk of insolvency leaves little room for a further premium to cover the risk of the loss and penalties of usury. The calculations of borrowers and lenders are not practically so nice. What do they care or know about the doctrine of chances ? The power of one side and the helplessness of the other fix the rates."

Judge Byles then proceeds to show how the repeal of the usury laws affects the landed interest, introducing uncertainty into the operations of mortgages, causing money to be called in when rates of interest take a rise, and imposing needless expense in new deeds and titles to estates already complex enough. Resolutions affecting the landed interest are generally slow and silent, but not the less sure. The Judge tells us, on the authority of the most eminent conveyancers, that one half of the landed property of the United Kingdom groans under incumbrances of debt of one kind or other.

APPENDIX K.

Proposed Exchequer Note.

" I promise to receive" instead of " I promise to pay."

It will be absolutely necessary to alter the tenor of the note if emancipation from the shackles of gold is to be looked for. The

The following specimen has been submitted to the Secretary of the Bank of England; but he declined to say whether it infringed 24 and 25 Vict., Cap. xcviii., Sec. 17, and referred the author to his own Solicitor:—

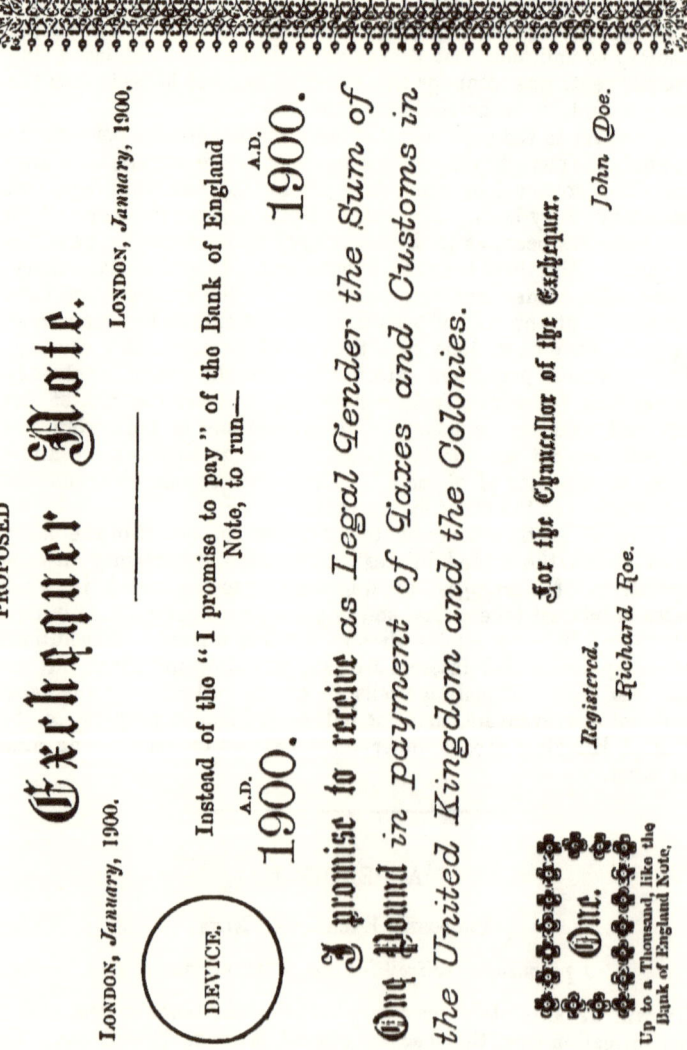

"promise to pay" of Mr. Pitt's one-pound note, like the "promise to pay" of the American Greenback, gave the gold advocates grounds for accusing both issues of want of faith. The following is given as a specimen of the note proposed to be issued. The promise is on the part of the Chancellor of the Exchequer to receive the note as quittance of taxation. As to a proposal that such issue should be imperial—that is, for the Colonies and India, —this is too bold to be more than hinted at at present; but nothing would tend more to conciliate the Colonies, and convert them into transmarine counties, than a money which should be legal tender through the Empire. We have high authority for the fact that the "SUPERSCRIPTION" is the outward and visible sign of imperial rule, and "ONE EMPIRE, ONE MONEY" is a principle worthy the grave consideration of statesmen.

The great want of the Colonies is money, and the miscellaneous circulation of Spanish dollars and other coins indicates this great want.

APPENDIX L.

SAMUEL JONES LOYD'S CYCLE.

THE following statement of the condition of the country, and especially of the labour market, under the different aspects of this cycle shows the oscillations between the one extreme of excitement, and the other of extreme depression.

"First we find trade in a state of quiescence—then of improvement — growing confidence — prosperity — excitement — over-trading — convulsion — pressure — stagnation — distress — ending again in quiescence."

THE LABOUR MARKET.

1837.

Depression after the panic of 1836.

After the excitement and over-trading of 1836, the report of the Manchester Chamber of Commerce bore witness to the ruin of fortunes, and also to the increase of disease, crime, and mortality.

At Leeds, Sheffield, Birmingham, Stockport, Huddersfield, Blackburn, and Bolton, the savings banks were drained by the depositors.

In Stafford, Nottingham, and Leicester, a cessation of the demand for labour.

In Coventry, Coleshill, Nuneaton, and Mansfield, the same industrial prostration.

1864.

Prosperity.

"Notwithstanding our experience of the vanity of prophecies and the fallibility of human speculations, it really seems hard to believe that the second year of the great Cotton Famine should actually have left the trade of this country more prosperous than before. We have been accustomed of late to see the most natural calculations refuted by events, but this result surpasses all former examples. Such, however, is the fact. We are doing more business in 1863 than we did in 1861, though in that year the dearth of cotton was scarcely felt.

"We need no further evidence to show how little we were dependent for our commercial prosperity on a single branch of trade, and yet our first inquiries on the subject are still naturally directed to our cotton manufactures. We cannot lose sight of an industry which was once so productive, and which we all hope to see productive again. In fact, it still occupies a prominent place in the official returns. The imports of raw material are very deficient, but the value of the manufactured exports has largely increased."—*Times.*

1867—1868—1869.

Depression after the panic of 1866.

The distress in the east of London still continues, and more than 1000 persons are relieved daily at the Soup Kitchens.

The distress has arisen from a variety of causes, but especially from the commercial panic of last year.

1867. "In closing our Review of 1866 we were compelled to describe it in somewhat unfavourable terms as a gloomy, unprosperous period. The events which stamped it with such a character were principally the severe commercial crisis, which produced widespread distress and commercial embarrassment, and a partially depressed harvest.

1868. "The shock given to confidence, the dulness of trade, and the stagnation of enterprise engendered by the calamitous failures of 1866 still exercised their paralysing influence upon the money market, and straitened the means of large classes of the community.

1869. "It was still matter of complaint that the depressing effect so long experienced upon trade by the commercial crisis of 1866 continued to be felt. The tardiness with which confidence revived was without parallel in the history of commercial revulsions, whilst the Chancellor of the Exchequer averred that " the revenue showed not the slightest symptom of elasticity."—*Annual Registers*.

1871.

Prosperity.

The general conclusion remains unaffected. Trade is active, and the country prosperous almost beyond example.

Cornish Mining.—" The dangerous excitement concerning the tin mines, and the recklessness displayed at the several weekly auctions for the sale of mine shares, have not been so marked since our last notice. Nevertheless, business has been done to the extent of many thousand pounds; at one auction nearly £6,000 worth of shares changed hands within a couple of hours. In some instances, prices, which had become outrageous, have given way consider-ably, and generally there has been a decline; but a further rise in the standards of ore—and a speedy improvement is generally expected—would in all probability materially renew the excitement, and send the prices higher. There is the utmost confidence that tin will command magnificent rates for a long time to come, and statistics certainly warrant the opinion as to firmness. Mines that were abandoned a few years ago are being set to work in all direc-tions, and at some of the revived undertakings most encouraging progress is being made. There is every prospect that Cornwall will soon materially increase her returns of tin. There is pressing demand for machinery for the new concerns, and many of the established miners are taking advantage of the prosperous times to increase and strengthen their machinery. Copper mines are also going ahead, and fresh and suspended works are being actively pushed forward with a view to greater supplies of mineral; £15 per ton is an important advance in price, and many points of operation will now pay for working which before the rise could only be dealt with for a loss. The returns of iron ore too, are increasing."—*Times*, 1871.

1872.

Prosperity.

" What are the signs of national prosperity? We have often asked that question, but, whatever the answer, we think just now there can be little mistake about the fact. For the 'upper ten thousand'—or, as it would be fairer to say of this country, the upper million—let London of to-day speak, crammed as it is beyond precedent with residents and visitors ready to take anything at any price, and anxious only for a chance of the bargain. Let public sales speak, where fifty pictures a day fetch each the value of fifty acres of good English land, and a couple of teacups will be bought in for a hundred guineas or so. Let subscription lists speak, in which thousands upon thousands are given for any object in any country under the sun. Perhaps the rejoinder will be that about the upper million no question need be raised or evidence tendered. Go a step lower, then, and look at the activity of trade in all its departments, the price of every article of produce, the condition of the money market, and above all, the gathering of the eagles above the carcases. There is good provender be sure in the shape of capital, when adventures are spread in such abundance before the eyes of capitalists, and we are once more, perhaps, on the eve of the 'mania' which precedes a panic. Take, again, the public expenditure and revenue—the one so large that it has been denounced as essentially intolerable, the other so elastic and so easily raised that people hardly trouble themselves about the matter. There used to be a never-failing protest at this stage of the story, but even that cannot be sustained now. The working classes are getting their share of good things at a rate never before witnessed. The rise in the value of labour is so universal and so extraordinary that it has now its regular place in the estimates of the largest employers in the world—the railway companies. Profits which have hitherto gone to shareholders are being shared by servants, and not unjustly. It seems to be a question whether next month's dividends will be maintained at the rate ruling in January, notwithstanding the buoyancy of the traffic and the exuberance of receipts. If we are reminded of yet another stratum of society, we answer that pauperism, too, is on the decline, and that the very poor and needy are fewer than they were."—*Times.*

The Unprecedented State of the Iron Trade.—"Although the present unprecedented prices in the iron trade are checking orders from all parts of the world, and though in Europe and America local works are now able to compete profitably with certain of our productions, our makers are in many cases so full of orders that they are unwilling to bind themselves to deliver before the year 1874. The fuel difficulty is in a measure relieved, but there are fears of further efforts among the colliers to reduce the hours of labour. The supply is already very deficient, and any further curtailment of the output would seriously embarrass many of the manufacturers. American advices mention that some small articles of hardware, which were formerly supplied from England, are now being made more cheaply in the States. The great mainstay of our iron trade, however, is heavy goods, especially railway material, and this is in increasing demand from all parts of the world, at still advancing prices."—*Financier.*

" *Barnsley.*—Ironworks more active. Men more settled. Plenty of work at the collieries.

"*Barrow-in-Furness.*—Foundries and engineering establishments well employed.

" *Birmingham.*—Scarcity of fuel felt, otherwise all well engaged.

" *Bradford.*—Machinery fully employed.

" *Cardiff.*—Colliers working with more regularity.

" *Dewsbury.*—Dyers and finishers fully employed.

" *Dudley.*—Mills and forges only in partial operation, fuel being scarce.

" *Dundee.*—Manufacturers fairly employed.

" *Forest of Dean.*—Colliers still unsettled. Fuel scarce.

" *Glasgow.*—Ship-building unwontedly active. Agitation amongst brass founders for shorter hours.

" *Halifax.*—Market firmer.

" *Huddersfield.*—Manufacturers well occupied.

" *Leeds.*—Strike of flax operatives.

" *Leicester.*—Elastic web manufacturers busy. Hosiers well employed. Boot and shoe trade steady.

" *Manchester.*—Market dull.

" *Merthyr.*—Collieries worked night and day. Ironworks continue active.

" *Middlesborough.*—Abundance of work amongst shipbuilders and engineers. Ironworks on the increase.

" *Newcastle-on-Tyne.*—Collieries, ironworks, and shipyards well engaged.

" *Newport (Mon.)*—Ironworks well employed.

" *Nottingham.*—Lace manufacturers actively employed ; prospects good. Hosiers fairly employed.

" *Sheffield.*—All ironworks (light and heavy) brisk. Several new works in progress.

" *Stoke-on-Trent.*—Works continue to be well employed. Colliers more settled.

" *Swansea.*—Abundance of work and good wages for all able and willing to work. Scarcity of colliers."

1875—1876—1877.

Continued depression.

After the excitement and over-trading of 1871 and 1872, " complaints were received from all parts of the kingdom. The Atlantic and South Pacific steamers, many of them laid up in ordinary.

" The London and North-Western Railway Company dismissed 400 men from the Crewe Works.

" Middlesborough, a week of profound anxiety and disquietude.

"The commercial atmosphere in the north of England is very depressing and unsatisfactory, and full of rumours which tend to banish confidence and constrain credit. Business is almost at a standstill, and then a list of failures."—*Engineer*.

"The *Times*, in a recent article, September 1876, ominously remarks, that '*all enterprise is dead.*' The italics are our own, but we claim to adopt a method of emphasis, for the observation is but the echo of a warning we have been giving ever since the beginning of the year 1875. All this time we have consistently and perseveringly endeavoured to impress upon our readers the true state to which our trade has been reduced, and we have done this to the manifest dislike of a large section of the mercantile world, such, for instance, as the money lender, pure and simple, the speculator, and the man who simply *wins* money but does not *make* it. We are glad now to find that the lesson is at length burned into the souls of men that trade is not remunerative. It is not convenient for certain parties that anyone should see that the gains of the money lenders are no longer drawn from the *profits* but from the *capital* of trade. Nevertheless, a vigorous modern writer has well remarked, all the lying lips of commercial Europe cannot conceal the facts much longer, and what the people will do to *Barabbas* when they find out at length that he is a robber and not a king, it is not for us to say.

"We have 'hard times' here in England, as unfortunately it is unnecessary to inform my readers; they know the painful fact too well. We shall have 'harder times,' for the optimists of the City themselves have admitted that trade is *dead*—not dying, mark, but *dead*, absolutely *dead*. The times are also hard in America, of whom alarmists are afraid, because they imagine that our 'cute kinsmen will take our trade from us. Perhaps depression of trade is even worse in America than here, and there are many in that country particularly, who believe that the great financial crash which is imminent will occur first in the United States and thence will spread to Great Britain."—*Monetary Gazette*, Sept. 1876.

APPENDIX M.

HOARDING.

IF paper money were adopted by any country, the insane practice of hoarding would be annihilated, to the discouragement of avarice. The miser, attaching value rather to the symbol than to the signification and powers of these discs of shining and beautiful metal, (the power consisting in the command it gives over other men's labour), is apt to store them up and feast his eyes with rows of sovereigns arranged in order, (this is depicted in the famous picture of the "Two Misers"), but would he derive the same pleasure in contemplating piles of paper notes? What man prides himself particularly on his bill case? But let him produce a bag of gold, and his very office boy gloats on the substantial treasure. The love of gold is, in fact, a relic of barbarism, only worthy of the half-civilized orientals.

It is this fanatical worship which induced our Henry the Seventh to hoard up treasure, which his son quickly dissipated in "the Field of the Cloth of Gold." These immense accumulations are injurious to the nation, who are deprived of their instrument of exchange—their legal tender—to gratify an absurd craving of the ruler. Thus we hear of the Emperor of Morocco collecting the very gold in which his subjects are bound to pay their taxes, and bricking it up in vaults. The Shah of Persia is guilty of the same folly; but a more recent and flagrant instance is the Minister of the Treasury in the United States of America, who actually proposes to hoard up gold to meet the demand which the resort to cash payments in 1878 will inevitably create,—a policy which must inflict incalculable distress on that once flourishing and happy Republic, which, if persisted in, will lead to popular commotion, if not to the secession of the Western States.

APPENDIX O.

English Money Sunk in Foreign Loans.

Mr. Mechi tells us "that £100,000,000 might easily be spent on improving these inferior soils, but the fiat of the professors of political economy has gone forth, and the results are shown above. Any foreign financier has only to promise 8, 9, or 10 per cent., and the easily gulled annuitant class gorges the bait. With the money thus thrown away, England might have been brought up to garden cultivation, estuaries embanked, bogs and marshes reclaimed, arterial drainage carried out, and sewage utilised, whilst the expenditure, being chiefly devoted to wages, would have helped to solve the pauper problem.

English Charities Abroad.—The Cosmopolitan Press Agency gives the following lists of the countries and states who have condescended to honour England by borrowing some of her superfluous pocket money, and who, moreover, have not yet thought it worth their while to reimburse her:—Turkey, principal unredeemed, £197,890,245; interest overdue, £11,423,593. Peru, principal unredeemed, £32,953,000; interest overdue, £2,638,599. Mexico, principal unredeemed, £27,905,800 ; interest overdue, £9,388,580. Venezuela, principal unredeemed, £6,616,800 ; interest overdue, £2,817,862. Virginia, principal unredeemed, £5,521,320 ; interest overdue, £698,732. Honduras, principal unredeemed, £5,398,570 ; interest overdue, £2,010,619. Costa Rica, principal unredeemed, £3,304,000 ; interest overdue, £471,972. Bolivia, principal unredeemed, £1,654,000 ; interest overdue, £198,480. Alabama, principal unredeemed, £1,444,000 ; interest overdue, £462,080. Ecuador, principal unredeemed, £1,824,000 ; interest overdue, £164,160. Greece, principal unredeemed, £2,400,000 ; interest overdue, £6,192,000. Guatemala, principal unredeemed, £542,200 ; interest overdue, £51,874. Liberia, principal unredeemed, £100,000 ; interest overdue, £21,000. Louisiana, principal unredeemed, £4,487,000 ; interest overdue, £916,000. Paraguay, principal unredeemed, £1,505,400 ; interest overdue, £331,188. San Domingo, principal unredeemed, £714,300 ; interest overdue, £192,861. Uruguay, principal unredeemed, £3,164,800 ; interest overdue, £189,888. Total, £335,094,423.—*Weekly Times*, *2nd March.*

APPENDIX P.

THE CURRENCY QUESTION IN WILLIAM III.'S REIGN.

LORD MACAULAY'S " History of England " is as popular a work as ever came out on the subject, and has been the cause of a diffusion of knowledge, which no other work ever effected. Its fault of brilliant rhetoric of unmitigated praise and blame, though little satisfactory to men of solid judgment, does not prevent Englishmen from relishing its fine writing in the free library of the great towns, or an Australian hut. But Lord Macaulay is the Whig historian, and, like his party, is devoted to bullionism and the monied interest, and he thus boldly propounds as self-evident axioms those fallacies exposed in the body of this work.

" These politicians whose voice was for delay gave less trouble than another set of politicians, who were for a general and immediate recoinage, but who insisted that *the new shilling should be worth only ninepence or ninepence halfpenny.* At the head of this party was William Lowndes, Secretary of the Treasury, and member of Parliament for Seaford, a most respectable and industrious servant, but much more versed in the details of office than in the higher parts of political philosophy. He was not in the least aware that *a piece of metal with the King's head on it was a commodity of which the price was governed by the same laws which govern the price of a piece of metal fashioned into a spoon or buckle,* and that it was no more in the power of Parliament to make the kingdom richer by calling a crown a pound, than to make a kingdom larger by calling a furlong a mile." (Vol. ii. p. 633.)

" *He* " (*Mr. Lowndes*) " *seriously believed, incredible as it may seem, that if the ounce of silver were divided into seven shillings instead of five, foreign nations would sell us their wines and silks for a smaller number of ounces.* " (Vol. ii., p. 632).

" He had a considerable following, composed partly of dull men, who really believed what he told them, and partly of shrewd men who were perfectly willing to be authorised by law to pay a hundred pounds with eighty." (Vol. ii. p. 633.)

" Had his arguments prevailed, the evils of a vast confiscation would have been added to all the other evils which afflicted the nation. Public credit, still in its tender and sickly infancy, would have been destroyed ; and there would have been much risk of a general mutiny of the fleet and army. Happily, Lowndes was completely refuted by Locke in a paper drawn up for the use of Somers. Somers was delighted with this little treatise, and desired that it might be printed. It speedily became the text-book of the most enlightened politicians in the kingdom, and may still be read with pleasure and profit. The effect of Locke's forcible and per-spicuous reasoning is greatly heightened by his evident anxiety to get at the truth, and by the singularly generous and graceful courtesy with which he treats an antagonist of powers far inferior to his own. Flamsteed, the Astronomer Royal, described the con-troversy well by saying that the point in dispute was whether five was six or only five.

" Thus far Somers and Montague entirely agreed with Locke, but as to the manner in which the restoration of the currency ought to be effected there was some difference of opinion. Locke recom-mended that the King should by proclamation fix a near day after which the hammered money should in all payments *pass only by weight*. The advantages of this plan were doubtless great and obvious. It was most simple, and at the same time most efficient. What searching, fining, branding, hanging, burning had failed to do would be done in an instant. The clipping of the hammered pieces, the melting of the milled pieces would cease. Great quantities of good coin would come forth from secret drawers, and from behind the panels of wainscots. The mutilated silver would gradually flow into the Mint, and would come forth again in a form which would make mutilation impossible. *In a short time the whole currency of the realm would be in a sound state*, and during the pro-gress of this great change there would never at any moment be any scarcity of money.

" These were weighty considerations ; and to the joint authority of North and Locke on such a question great respect is due. Yet it must be owned that their plan was open to one serious objection, which did not indeed altogether escape their notice, but of which they seem to have thought too lightly. The restoration of the currency was a benefit to the whole community. On what principle then was the expense of restoring the currency to be borne by a part of the community? It was most desirable, doubtless, that the words pound and shilling should again have a fixed signification, that every man should know what his contracts meant, and what his property was worth. But was it just to attain this excellent end, by means of which the effect would be, that every farmer who had put by a hundred pounds to pay his rent, every trader who had scraped together a hundred pounds to meet his acceptances, would find his hundred pounds reduced in a moment to fifty or sixty? It was not the fault of such a farmer, or of such a trader, that his crowns or half-crowns were not of full weight. The Government itself was to blame. The evil which the State had caused the State was bound to repair; and it would evidently have been wrong to throw the charge of the reparation on a particular class merely because that class was so situated that it could conveniently be pillaged. It would have been as reasonable to require the timber merchants to bear the whole cost of fitting out the Channel Fleet, or the gunsmiths to bear the whole cost of supplying arms to the regiments in Flanders, as to restore the currency of the kingdom at the expense of those individuals in whose hands the clipped silver at a particular moment happened to be.

" Locke declared that he regretted the loss which, if his advice were taken, would fall on the holders of the short money. But it appeared to him that the nation must make a choice between evils. And, in truth, it was much easier to lay down the general proposition, that the expenses of restoring the currency ought to be borne by the public, than to devise any mode in which they could, without extreme inconvenience and danger, be so borne. Was it to be announced that every person who should within a year or half a year carry to the Mint a clipped crown should receive in exchange for it a milled crown, and that the difference between the value of the two pieces should be made good out of the public purse? That would be to offer a premium for clipping. The shears would be more busy than ever. The short money would every day become shorter. The difference which the tax-payer would have to make good would probably be greater by a million at the end of the term than at the beginning : and the whole of this million would go to reward malefactors. If the time allowed for bringing in the hammered coin were much shortened, the danger of further clipping would be proportionately diminished ; but another danger would be incurred. The silver would flow into the Mint so much faster than it could possibly flow out that there must be during some months a grievous scarcity of money.

" A singularly bold and ingenious expedient occurred to Somers, and was approved by William. It was that a proclamation should be prepared with great secrecy, and published at once through all parts of the kingdom. This proclamation was to announce that hammered coin would henceforth *pass only by weight*. The very possessor of such coins was to be invited to deliver them up within three days in a sealed packet, to the public authorities. The coins were to be examined, numbered, weighed, and returned to the owner with a promissory note, entitling him to receive from the Treasury at a future time the difference between the actual quantity of silver in his pieces, and the quantity of silver which, according to the standard, those pieces ought to have contained ! Had this plan been adopted an immediate stop would have been put to the clipping, the melting, *and the exporting* ; and the expense of the restoration of the currency would have been borne, as was right, by the public. The inconvenience arising from a scarcity of money would have been of very short duration, for the multilated pieces would have been detained only till they could have been told and weighed : they would have been sent back into circulation, and the recoinage would have taken place gradually, and without any perceptible suspension or disturbance of trade. But against these great advantages were to be set off hazards, which Somers was prepared to brave, but from which it is not strange that politicians of less elevated character should have shrunk. The course which he recommended to his colleagues was indeed the safest for the country, but by no means was the safest for themselves. This plan could not be successful unless the execution were sudden ; the execution could not be sudden if the previous sanction of Parliament were asked and obtained ; and to take a step of such fearful importance without the previous sanction of Parliament was to run the risk of censure, impeachment, imprisonment, and ruin. The King and the Lord Keeper were alone in the council. Even Montague quailed, and it was determined to do nothing without the authority of the legislature. Montague undertook to submit to the Commons a scheme which was not indeed without dangers and inconveniences, but which was probably the best which he could hope to carry.

"Since the Revolution the state of the currency had been repeatedly discussed by Parliament. In 1689, a committee of the Commons had been appointed to investigate the subject, but had made no report. In 1690, another committee had reported that immense quantities of silver were carried out of the country by Jews, who, it was said, would do anything for profit. Schemes were formed for encouraging the importation and discouraging the exportation of the precious metals. One foolish Bill after another was brought in and dropped. At length, in the beginning of the year 1695, the question assumed so serious an aspect that the Houses applied themselves to it in earnest. The only practical result of their deliberations, however, was a new penal law, which, it was hoped, would prevent the *clipping of the hammered coin and the melting and exporting of the milled coin.* It was enacted that every person who informed against a clipper should be entitled to forty pounds; that every clipper that informed against two clippers should be entitled to a pardon ; and that whoever should be found in possession of silver filings or parings should be burned in the cheek with a red-hot iron.

"But, happily for England, there were among her rulers some who clearly perceived that it was not by halters and branding-irons that her decaying industry and commerce could be restored to health. The state of the currency had, during some time, occupied the serious attention of four eminent men, closely connected by public and private ties. Two of them were politicians, who had never, in the midst of official and parliamentary business, ceased to love and honour philosophy; and two were philosophers, in whom habits of abstruse meditation had not impaired the homely good sense without which even genius is mischievous in politics. Never had there been an occasion which more urgently required both practical and speculative abilities, and never had the world seen the highest practical and speculative abilities united in an alliance so close, so harmonious, and so honourable as that which bound Somers and Montague to Locke and Newton.

"Adam Smith has often been justly blamed for maintaining, in direct opposition to all his own principles, that *the rate of interest ought to be regulated by the State;* and he is the more blamable because, long before he was born, both Locke and North had taught that it was *as absurd to make laws fixing the price of money as to make laws fixing the price of cutlery or of broadcloth; but who insisted that the new shilling should be worth only ninepence or ninepence halfpenny?"—History of England*, Vol. iv. p. 632.

Mr. Lowndes, a practical man, sa was clearly as Bishop Berkely that the shilling in its character of token did not depend on the intrinsic value of a coin,—did not depend on the quantity of silver contained in the shilling, but on the money denomination conferred on it by the act of coining. The end, aim, and purpose of coining in the State mint is, to give it that money denomination which constituted it legal tender to the amount of forty shillings, which made it the twentieth part of a sovereign, or, in those days, the twenty-first part of a guinea, and worth twelve pence in copper.

It may seem presumptuous to expose errors of such men as Locke and Newton, but, like our philosophers in 1819, they were misled by the common prejudice that money must have intrinsic value,—a prejudice, according to Bishop Berkely, their contemporary, "entertained by the vulgar of all ranks." Our practical men in 1819, like Mr. Lowndes, saw the error, but were overpowered by a literary and philosophical clique backed by popular ignorance.

Lord Macaulay does not see that money is an instrument for carrying on internal trade,—for the payment of taxes and debts,—for the till, the purse, and, above all, for wages ;—that it does not enter into foreign trade, which is barter,—so much hardware, earthenware, etc., for so much " wine and silk ; " and not seeing this his comments are worthless.

" These were weighty considerations, and to the joint authority of Locke and North on such a question great respect is due. Yet it must be owned that their plan was open to one serious objection, which did not altogether escape their notice, but of which they seem to have thought too lightly. The restoration of the currency was a benefit to the whole community.

" *On what principle then was the expense of restoring the currency to be borne by a part of the community? It was most desirable, doubtless, that the words pound and shilling should again have a fixed signification, that every man should know what his contracts meant and what his property was worth.*"—*History of England*, v. ii. p. 634.

The difficulties in which this false principle landed them accumulated. They did not see that the " words pound and shilling had a fixed signification." They did not see that the money denomination had given them " that fixed signification." This was illustrated by Mr. Gladstone's bronze coinage. He reduced the penny one-third in weight, and by proclamation in the *Gazette* made the new coin of the same value as the old one, and they were at once received into circulation by the people without the least demur, nay, with great satisfaction, at having a light portable disc of bronze. It was in utter ignorance that Lord Liverpool issued the old penny of an ounce weight; the consequence was that when copper rose in value in the open market the dealers in copper melted them, regardless of fine and imprisonment; one of his reasons was that the penny might serve as an ounce weight as well as a coin ! Absurdity could no farther go.

"In 1690 another committee had reported that immense quantities of silver were carried out of the country by Jews, who, it was said, would do anything for profit. Schemes were formed for encouraging the importation and discouraging the exportation of the precious metals."

The false principle at work! If the silver had had a conventional value given to it,—"if the ounce of silver had been divided into seven shillings instead of five," the Jews would never have touched it.

But Mr. Locke was well aware that there was something wrong

at the very root of metallic money, for in his work he thus shows the consequences of a restricted supply of money, without apparently being aware that a gold currency must necessarily be restricted :—

" If one-third of the money were locked up, the people, not perceiving the money to be gone, would be jealous one of another, and each would employ his skill and power the best he could to retrieve it again and bring it back to his pocket in the same plenty as before. But this is but scrambling among ourselves, and helps no more against our wants than the pulling of a short coverlet will, among children that lie together, preserve them all from the cold. Some will starve unless the father provide better and enlarge the scanty covering."—*John Locke.*

Rightly interpreted, this parable refers to the Government, which is recommended " to provide better," and to the people, who are likened to " children scrambling with each other for a share of the short coverlet." But under the metallic system the coverlet must inevitably be short, and the remedy, a larger coverlet, can only be acquired through an expansive State paper based on labour and not on gold.

APPENDIX Q.

Andrew Yarranton in 1677.

CAPITALISTS BECOMING A LANDED ARISTOCRACY.

That country gentlemen have been cruelly robbed by the usurious exactions of monied men has been noticed by writers in old times. The seizure of the treasure of the Goldsmith's Company by Charles II. roused the attention of such men as Roger North, John Lowndes of the Treasury, and Andrew Yarranton. This latter, as early as 1677, in his " England's Improvement by Sea and Land— to outdo the Dutch without Fighting ; to Pay Debts without Money; to set at Work all the Poor of England with the Growth of our own Lands, etc.,"—describes the difficulty of raising money, and how a landed gentleman, who wished to borrow on the security of his estate, was gradually engulphed in ruin by the exactions of money scriveners, aided by lawyers, who to this day oppose the registration of land, which he strongly advocates. He wrote :—

" But it will be objected that I am no friend to the way of banking as it now is. I do profess it, and have been of the same mind this ten years last past, and have declared before some of the bankers, and many persons of quality besides, that this way of banking would endanger the kingdom. And when I saw it convenient, which was in January last, I gave reasons in public coffee houses for my opinion, some of the bankers being present. Their way of dealing I knew, and what security they took, which was impossible should run long. And as the land and personal security is at this day, no living man, though never so knowing in the laws or in men, can take a great cash in his hands, and pay six in the hundred for it. Is it not a sad thing that a banker's boy should take up more monies upon his notes in one day, than two lords, four knights, and eight esquires in twelve months, upon all their personal securities? We cannot expect this from any of our neighbours abroad, whose interest depends upon our loss. Were it not much better that those lords, knights, and esquires that now pay eight, nine, and ten pounds for their monies, and are contented to sell their lands at sixteen years' purchase, after lawsuits, and troubles attending the law have destroyed the one-half, should bring up their lands to thirty years' purchase, and monies down to three-and-a-half in the hundred, and redeem the old credit paid by the people to them?

"As it is, the gentleman is obliged to borrow money at exorbitant interest, and now his miseries come on,—what must he do? His creditors come upon him; the charge of law-suits comes on; his affairs are distracted. I tell you what some have done,—either turn over to the Fleet or the Bench. Oh, pity and sin, that it should be so in brave England! First, pity that a poor gentleman cannot have money at such interest upon his land as the law directs, to pay his just debts, and for the good comfort of his family. And, secondly, it is a sin that a gentleman of £1,000 a year should ruin so many families by putting them to vexatious suits for their money lent."—*England's Improvement.*

The landed gentry should open their eyes to the insidious arts of the monied men, who are encroaching year by year on the old families, whom they are rapidly displacing. The chief agent in this transfer is that deadly instrument, wielded by the *duumvirate* —the man of money, and the lawyer—the mortgage. Look which way you will and this work is going on, and the last resort of the harassed and bankrupt landed gentry, the squirarchy, and the old families, is to sacrifice the happiness and self-respect of their sons and daughters, and seek matrimonial alliances with this rapacious, cunning, and unscrupulous body. English history, down to the time of the Tudors, abounds with these alliances between blood and money. The battle between the two aristocracies might excite but a languid interest; but unfortunately the people suffer from the ceaseless, unremitting, law-protected exactions of these usurers, rapidly becoming our landlords, a process in full operation in America at this day.—(*V.* p. 89.)

By virtue of an act, 24, V.R.,
c. 5, dated at the
Exchequer.

(DEVICE.)

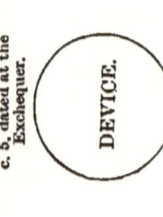

(DEVICE.)

By virtue of an act 24, V.R.,
c. 5, dated at the
Exchequer.

Form of Exchequer Bill.

£1,000.

This Exchequer Bill entitles*

or order, to claim payment of ONE THOUSAND POUNDS, at the Bank of England, out of the Consolidated Fund, at the expiration of any period of Twelve Months, not later than Five Years, from the date hereof.

Interest† on this Bill will be paid half-yearly at the Bank of England, at such rate per centum per annum as shall be notified from time to time in the "London Gazette," by the Commissioners of Her Majesty's Treasury.

This Bill may be paid, for the sum of ONE THOUSAND POUNDS and Interest accrued thereon, to the Receivers and Collectors in the United Kingdom, of any of the public Revenues, Aids, Taxes, or Supplies, or to the account of Her Majesty's Exchequer at the Bank of England, at any time in the last six months of every year, commencing from the day of the date hereof, in which it shall have currency by law.

Signed in the presence of
H. W. CHURCHILL.

N.B.—The Cheques must not be mutilated.

* If this blank is not filled up this Bill will be paid to bearer.
† Interest payable to holder of Exchequer Bill averages about 3d. a day per £100.

APPENDIX S.

MARCO POLO'S DESCRIPTION OF THE GRAND KHAN'S SYSTEM OF PAPER MONEY.

THE following is the account of the mode of making, authenticating, and issuing Paper Money by the Grand Khan, as described by Marco Polo :—

"In this city of Kanbalu is the mint of the Grand Khan, who may truly be said to possess the secret of the alchymists, as he has the art of producing money by the following process. He causes the bark to be stripped from the mulberry trees, the leaves of which are used for feeding silkworms, and takes from it that thin inner rind which lies between the coarser bark and the wood of the tree.

"This being steeped, and afterwards pounded in a mortar until reduced to a pulp, is made into paper, resembling (in substance) that which is manufactured from cotton, but quite black. When ready for use, he has it cut into pieces of money of different sizes, nearly square, but somewhat longer than they are wide. Of these, the smallest pass for a *denier tournois;* the next size for a Venetian silver groat, others for two, five, or ten groats; others for one, two, and three, and as far as ten *bisants* of gold. The coinage of this Paper Money is authenticated with as much form and ceremony as if it were actually of pure gold or silver; for to each note a number of officers specially appointed, not only subscribe their names, but affix their signets also ; and when this has been regularly done by the whole of them, the principal officer deputed by his Majesty, having dipped into vermilion the royal seal committed to his custody, stamps with it the piece of paper, so that the form of the seal tinged with the vermilion remains impressed upon it, by which it receives full authenticity as current money, and the act of counterfeiting is punished as a capital offence. When thus coined in large quantities, this paper currency is circulated in every part of his Majesty's dominions, nor dare any person at the peril of his life refuse to accept it as payment. All his subjects receive it without hesitation, because wherever their business may call them, they can dispose of it again in the purchase of merchandise they have occasion for, such as pearls, jewels, gold, or silver. With it, in short, every article may be procured."—*Marsden's "Travels of Marco Polo,"* p. 353.

APPENDIX T.

THE following is a specimen of the broadsheets stereotyped and circulating in America by the thousand. The writer, the Rev. E. Palmer, of Amby, N. J., denounces usury from the pulpit.

Righteousness the only Security for Free Institutions.

Usury.—The term usury primarily signified what is now called "interest on money." Until within a comparatively modern period no attempt was made to legalize the requiring of a certain per cent., making all more than that illegal. For many centuries the requiring of any premium, however small, for money loaned, was regarded as unjust and oppressive.

Money, in its primitive and true character, is a certificate of service, as well as a medium of exchange; a measure of individual merit; justly loaned by one to another, only as a token of *confidence*, or *worthiness of credit;* never to be prostituted, as it now is, by being loaned for a *price.* He who does it, lowers his own character, obscures his moral vision, and compromises with iniquity.

It is a base perversion, and violation of moral principle, to make merchandise of money; to hold it in the market as a commodity, the price to be determined by the "law of supply and demand;" the anti-Christian law by which unprincipled men make others' necessity their opportunity for the practice of extortion and injustice.

Usury, in its ordinary form, is what one man requires of another, for the use of that which *he* does not want to use; while he has ample security for the faithful return of it in every way as good as new. If the circumstances of the borrower, through sickness or from any other cause, be such as to make it necessary for the time of the loan to be very much extended, though the lender may not have wanted it during the whole period, the borrower is required, not only to return what he borrowed, all as good as ever, but *twice as much.*

Or, if in the course of a long number of years, the borrower shall have returned, out of his hard earnings, a portion every year, until he shall have returned the whole amount twice over, that is for *usury*, and counts nothing. He is still required to pay again the whole of the original amount, even though it strip him of all that is left of the product of his labour, and leaves him, in his old age, houseless and destitute. This is an every-day occurrence, an ordinary business transaction. It is only *one* of the many ways by which usury sponges up all the net product of labour, passes it into the hands of the few, and leaves the toiling millions in poverty. The process by which it is perpetrated, to give it more plausibility in these latter days, is called *interest.* It is a *mistaken* interest, to say the least of it; for it cannot be the *true* interest of any so utterly to disregard the true interest of others.

It is this false and mistaken interest which holds men in such false and conflicting relations with each other. The true interests of each and all men are *harmonious*, because they are *just;* while this false interest, because it is false and *unjust*, is in conflict with the true interests of all men. It has so inverted the divine order, that under its influence men not only find themselves in conflict with each other, but literally in conflict with the product of their own hands. It has instigated a direct and positive hostility between LABOUR and CAPITAL; which would otherwise be in friendly, mutually beneficial, and harmonious relations. It has given to capital a centralizing power by which it holds labouring men in such complete subjection that the perpetual poverty of the labouring class is inevitable.

In plain terms, it is a system of *legalized robbery*. And it is not the most honourable kind of robbery; for it takes most from that class who are least able to part with it. It is literally *picking the pockets* of the poor toiling millions, who are rendered hopeless, and morally powerless, by the excessive labour to which it subjects them. It *causes*, *increases*, and *perpetuates* their poverty and degradation.

The demoralizing effects of such a system are *incalculable*. The flood of iniquity which has come in upon us through this ungodly source, and the (suffering which inevitably follows, cannot be *conceived* by finite man. It is our imperative duty to be taking measures to put away from among us this prolific source of evil, before we are overwhelmed by its corrupting influences, which already threaten to engulf us in moral ruin.

It becomes us to look to it in season, and see that we are doing our duty in the way of enlightening these men, and showing them how the wrong under which they are suffering is to be righted by moral means, peacefully and legitimately, and not by physical force, violence, and bloodshed.

Friends of Humanity.—It is evident that the next great step for ameliorating the condition of mankind is the establishment of a truly just and righteous MONETARY SYSTEM. *We must have a radical and thorough Financial Reform.* A true and thorough financial reform will inevitably lead to a true and thorough reform in everything; for everything in the civilized world is now controlled by the *Money Power*. Not only controlled, but perverted, prostituted, almost subverted by it. The wickedness of the Money Power, its unlimited potency for evil, will be found to be in the *usury system;* a subtle system of falsehood of such mighty false power, that it overrules and falsifies all the affairs of men. It is only necessary that this specious and overpowering system of iniquity shall be known, its true character understood, and it will not be permitted any longer to wrong, pervert, degrade, and scourge mankind. .

The abolition of usury is essential to the salvation of the Republic. To purge it of what is false and corrupting; enforce just and proper economy; remove the temptation to excessive expenditure, and restrain the headlong tendency to extravagance and destruction. Securing the permanency of free institutions by establishing them upon the immovable foundation of absolute Right, equal and exact justice to all men.

Bankruptcy and repudiation, otherwise unavoidable, will by this reform be precluded. The immense sums which are swallowed up by usury, paying debts over and over again, and still leaving the bonds undiminished, these hundreds of thousands of millions will henceforth be applied to the payment of the debts, once and for ever, to the satisfaction of all just and honourable men.

In advocating this reform, it is not against *persons* that we are contending; but against a false *system*, which has been transmitted to us by past generations, and which now controls and governs all men.

Work to be Done.—A great reform is to be inaugurated to overcome and put an end to the most gigantic iniquity in the world. To educate the people up to the truth in relation to this enormous evil, ways and means are to be adopted adequate to the accomplishment of the work.

Among the first things necessary is *organization*. Societies are to be formed for the investigation and free discussion of the subject, in all its relations and bearings. Things which are not hath God chosen to bring to naught things that are.

The preachers of religion are to be appealed to, and urged to do their duty in the premises. If they or their parishioners are not ready to hear the truth, we must turn to the Gentiles; appeal to the common people, who will hear us gladly; through them the church will be reached, and its standard restored to its primitive elevation.

The question is not, How it will affect one or a few persons to give up usury, while all others hold on to the system with all its unrighteous advantages? But the question is, Would it not be an incalculable benefit to all mankind to have the system abolished, with all its concomitants of poverty, vice, degradation, and crime?

No DIVISION OF PROPERTY, or community of goods, is asked or needed. Justice is all that is necessary, and a spirit of fraternity will spontaneously follow. None are asked to give up any of their property or money; but simply to give up an old system of injustice, which is the source of incalculable evil and inconceivable suffering to the human family.

In the triumph of this great reform there is everything for true men to hope, and nothing to fear. As usury, with its false and perverting influence, has been so instrumental in corrupting mankind, so the Anti-Usury Reform will be instrumental in bringing them back to truth and righteousness, to regeneration and moral renovation.

All men are now in bondage; burdened with care and anxiety;

literally weary and heavy laden. The Anti-Usury Reform is the harbinger of universal emancipation. It is the harbinger of justice, and consequently of security, permanent prosperity, and everlasting peace.

All Suffer by Usury.—So little is understood of this giant iniquity that most persons suppose there are none really sufferers by it but those who hire money. In its various forms it reaches all classes and affects all persons, pecuniarily and morally.

The comparatively few who are so unrighteously made rich by it are more and more blinded and deluded as they are so unrighteously made richer; while the poor toiling millions are sadly wronged and degraded by it, in being so unrighteously made poorer.

Debt and Credit.—It is proposed by some to abolish the credit system, because of its false and perverting influence. But it will be found that this usury system is the life and source of all false credit, and is itself the most wicked, as it is the most unlimited, of all false credit systems. It is a false demand for the net product of all the labour of all labouring men and their heirs for ever. And what is still more discouraging, the harder they work and the more they produce, the more this false debt or demand is increased. The larger the amount of capital, of course, the greater amount of interest to be paid, and the more labour is required to pay it. So That the longer this system of falsehood and iniquity is continued, the more enormous this false debt or demand for future toil becomes against all working men and their successors, through all future time.

The American people have now an enormous national debt to pay; and in strict justice should pay it but once. A debt once paid ought to satisfy and will satisfy all just men. But the usury system demands that this enormous debt, the usury upon which amounts to about two hundred millions of dollars annually, shall thus be paid over and over again, and yet remain undiminished.

EXTRACT FROM A SPEECH BY MR. KUYKENDALL, OF ILLINOIS.

The Truth in Congress.—" HARDLY a day passes without the introduction of some measure looking to a change in our monetary laws, indicating the universal opinion that the present system is imperfect, if not radically wrong. The latter I hold to be true, and the bill which I introduce contemplates a thorough change in the financial policy of the Government, as well as important alterations in our revenue system.

" Among the chief objects for which governments are instituted is that of protecting the rights of property and securing its equitable distribution, according to the labour or service performed in its production. And no government, whether republican or not, that fails to effect these important ends, can permanently secure the prosperity and happiness of the people.

"It cannot be successfully denied that physical and intellectual labour employed in production, and in the distribution of the products of labour is the true and only source of national wealth, and that labourers, as a whole, are poor. Look where you will upon society, you will see those who build palatial residences living in hovels; those who manufacture the finest apparel, clothed in the coarsest fabrics; and those who produce in abundance the most wholesome and delicate food, subsisting upon the poorest diet; all deprived of the time and means necessary for social and intellectual culture, and to a great degree destitute of the ordinary comforts and conveniences of life; condemned to lives of unremunerated toil; while another class, few in number, not physically, intellectually, or morally better than the average of society, acquire the large portion of the products of labour, live in comparative idleness, surrounded with all the comforts, conveniences, and luxuries of life. Besides this evil of centralizing wealth in the possession of the few, every few years our country is visited with a monetary crisis, prostrating all branches of productive industry and legitimate enterprise, deranging commercial operations, retarding the development of our natural resources, preventing us from becoming self-sustaining and independent as a nation. This disparity in the conditions of society, these monetary crises and commercial disasters, are at one time attributed to over-production, another time to short production; again they are assigned to the want of sufficient tariff on imports or duties on foreign manufactures. We have greatly increased production by the invention of labour-saving machines, have raised and lowered tariffs without producing any permanent beneficial effects, unless it be the building up of a cotton-mill or iron aristocracy. The wealth continues to centralize in fewer hands; the number of industrious poor who own no real and little personal property continues to increase. None of the causes assigned have ever satisfactorily accounted for these wrongs or pointed to a remedy, because they do not reach the true source of the evil, which will be found in the unfair distribution of the products of labour between non-producing capital and producing labour caused by the institution of money on a wrong principle, and with too great power over labour and property."

During the centuries of transition, however, through which our civilization has been passing, and in which the governments of Europe have been the oppressors instead of the servants of the people, labour has been so ground down by taxes, the income from which went to support the extravagance of the rulers, that it has become despised. The strongest evidence of this is found in our language. We speak of the "working classes," the "labouring classes," as though it was right and natural that there should be classes which did not labour, did not work; as though industry was not as natural to man as to all created beings; as though it was not the foundation and necessary basis of an advance in culture and refinement.

While this is so, how can we expect anything but corruption in our politics, injustice in our legislation, frivolity in our literature, falsehood in our press, fraud and adulteration in commerce, the vulgarity and extravagance of fashion in society, and selfishness prevailing in all the relations of men? An idle brain is the devil's workshop.

It remains then for the labour of this country, by dignifying itself, to make the dignity of labour no longer a mockery.

Wealth must not be used as wealth is now used by those who get it in every other way than by honest labour. It must not be expended in the foolish display, the empty vanity, and the wicked extravagance of the idle, but as men conscious of the dignity and respectability of their position would want to spend it. By being industrious, by using the mental and physical powers which nature has given us, and only thus, we are carrying out the law of our being. And by using the wealth thus gained by industry, in securing and diffusing to the entire race of mankind the means of happiness, and the cultivation of all their physical, mental, and spiritual powers, we are equally carrying out the destiny of the race upon this planet.

There is nothing now wanting to make this a free and happy country but the proper adjustment of Capital and Labour, and the changes to which that will naturally lead.

Our Hope of Success.—The prospect of succeeding in this great reform may not look very encouraging from the world's point of view, but from the true Christian stand-point the prospect is bright and cheering. It is undoubtedly the purpose of God that this world shall be redeemed from iniquity, and all men brought into obedience to the truth. It is our highest privilege to be co-workers with Him in the accomplishment of this glorious work; and we know that our labour shall not be in vain.

APPENDIX U.

The Influence of Steam and Electricity.

BY F. THURBER, OF NEW YORK.

Extract from the " International Review."

These great factors have had an astounding commercial, political, and economical bearing upon life in the nineteenth century.

In no department of life has the influence of these great factors been greater than in that of commerce. Fifty years ago commerce was a crude, slow, and laborious interchange of products. A few persons controlled the principal staples in the markets of the world, and stored them until the consumer was obliged to pay the price asked for them. Now, the whole world has become producers or traders, and in the event of scarcity at a given place, the news is flashed to the point of supply—under the ocean and around the earth even—and the giant power of steam hurries the products of the world to our doors. In this we see how wonderfully the one power is supplemented and aided by the other; there is nothing yet discovered in creation so marvellous, and we must turn to fairy land for a parallel: the story of Aladdin and his Lamp is realized; steam is our "genie," and electricity our "slave of the ring"—the one has the power to remove mountains, the other to annihilate time and space.

Lord Bacon has said, "There be three things which make a nation great and prosperous: a fertile soil, busy workshops, and easy conveyance of men and things from place to place."

This was true at the time it was said, and is also true to-day; but with the advent of steam and electricity, and the consequent extension of the geographical limits of commerce, the latter condition has completely overshadowed the former; and at this time, the producing, manufacturing, and consuming interests, together with the mercantile or distributing interest, are all dependent upon and controlled by the transportation interest. The abuses which have crept into the management of our carrying system are among the causes of the present unsatisfactory state of trade throughout the United States, and have given rise to the general demand for some change that will prevent the many from being thus taxed for the benefit of the few. This brings us to

The Political Aspect of the Question,

and to properly understand it, we must go back and see how steam and electricity came to have anything to do with politics.

From time immemorial our highways were owned and kept in order by the people;* but when the vastly superior steam roads were invented, the people delegated their powers and duties in this respect to associations of individuals; and, being overjoyed at the coming of the great benefactor, they neglected to shut the door against attendant evils. With but little consideration they granted concessions without proper restrictions and safeguards, which soon made their possessors so powerful that by combination and consolidation they became, in many cases, monopolies, with

* In this country the King's Highway has been converted into the private property of companies, to whose hands is committed the entire power of intercommunication. The Railway would have been a sound basis for the issue of a Paper Money, and then remained the property of the nation.— . *II.* (p. 107).

power sufficient to prevent or crush competition, and to unduly tax and oppress the people who created them.

Let us examine this power. The latest statistics show that we have, in the United States, about 74,000 miles of railway, with a nominal capital of 4,200,000,000 dollars; their gross receipts aggregate over 500,000,000 dollars; amounts greatly in excess of the government debt and revenue; all this sum is capable of being controlled and directed by a very few men; on all questions where railroad interests conflict with the interest of the public, the influence of this wealth is a unit against the people. It employs great armies in operating the various lines of road; it is the best customer of the press; it controls the telegraph lines, has the readiest access to the public ear, and is the all-powerful abettor or terrible foe to political aspirations. Many of our laws are made in its interest, and along every line of railway it keeps in its employ the best legal talent; these men become our judges, and, having been educated to view laws relating to railway matters from a railway stand-point, naturally interpret difficult points in its favour. Members of the legal profession are often in the lobby to serve this interest; and instances are not wanting where representatives of the people, while holding official positions, accept retainers to advocate claims adverse to the rights of the people. A railroad corporation is soulless, and yet immortal; wiser than philosophy, it has found in a perpetual charter the elixir of life. When our fathers abolished the law of primogeniture, they supposed the country was secured against the evils of vast individual wealth accumulating from generation to generation, because the certainty of death would bring the certainty of distribution; but a perpetual charter, granted without consideration, has become a spindle to twist the gossamer thread across the chasm of death. All this vast and constantly increasing wealth is under irresponsible control. A corporation can neither be hung nor sent to the penitentiary; * that is to say, there is an entire absence of individual responsibility. Vigorous, alert, all-powerful, and perpetual, it only needs unscrupulous managers to become a worse tyrant than Nero—a more dangerous master than Robespierre. On page 158 of the Report of the United States Senate Committee on Transportation Routes, we find the following:—

"In the matter of taxation, there are to-day four men, representing the four great trunk lines between Chicago and New York, who possess, and not unfrequently exercise, powers which the Congress of the United States would not venture to exert. They may at any time, and for any reason satisfactory to themselves, by a single stroke of the pen, reduce the value of property in this

---

* More pithily, but coarsely expressed by the popular saying, "that a corporation has neither a body to be kicked, nor a soul to be saved."—*J. H.*

country by hundreds of millions of dollars. An additional charge of five cents per bushel on the transportation of cereals would have been equivalent to a tax of 45,000,000 dollars on the crop of 1873. No Congress would dare to exercise so vast a power, except upon a necessity of the most imperative nature; and yet these gentlemen exercise it whenever it suits their supreme will and pleasure, without explanation or apology. With the rapid and inevitable progress of combination and consolidation, these colossal organizations are daily becoming stronger and more imperious. The day is not distant, if it has not already arrived, when it will be the duty of the statesman to inquire whether there is less danger in leaving the property and the industrial interests of the people thus wholly at the mercy of a few men, who recognize no responsibility but to their stockholders, and no principle of action but personal and corporate aggrandizement, than in adding somewhat to the power and patronage of a government directly responsible to the people, and entirely under their control."

While the construction of railways has extended over a period of forty-five years, about 44,000 miles have been finished within the last fifteen years; many of them were projected and built far in advance for the wants of the country, solely for the subsidies of public lands and money which have been lavishly given, and for the profit of rings known as "construction companies"—the directors in the railroad company letting to themselves, as a construction company, the contract for building the road at one price, then reletting it to *bona fide* contractors at half the price they obtained, the contractors in some instances reletting to subcontractors. The Union and Central Pacific roads were built in this manner, and the history of the construction company of the former road, known as the "Crédit mobilier," is familiar to every one; the history of the legislation, however, by which this road was projected and built, may not be so familiar, and we will give a brief summary.

As a premium for the building of the Central Pacific railroad, Congress passed an act granting the company twelve millions of acres of the public lands—an area the size of which can be appreciated when we say that it is one-third larger than the combined States of Massachusetts, Rhode Island, and Connecticut. Having secured this, the company represented that they were unable to finish the road unless they were given the right to issue and dispose of first mortgage bonds; and they introduced and lobbied through Congress an act changing the mortgage held by the government from a first to a second lien, when they immediately proceeded to issue bonds and stock, the proceeds of which the "Crédit mobilier" was formed to divide.

The foregoing history is interesting chiefly in showing how great corporations manage to mould and shape legislation to suit their ends, and in this respect the history of the Union Pacific, in its inflation and false statement of costs, finds a counterpart in that of most of the other roads throughout the United States. Nearly every State Legislature has had the same experience; an examination of the legislation of the past twenty years will show that the railroads have had pretty much their own way, and that legislatures, either by sins of omission or commission, have sadly neglected to protect the public interest.

When it becomes the interest of unscrupulous men to perpetuate these abuses they become politicians. And, to our shame be it said, so many of our railway managers are of that class, and so often is political influence in demand to serve their purposes, that in many parts of our country the entire patronage of these powerful organizations is bent to that end, and the political management of railways has become a science.

One great feature, however, of their politics is, that they never quarrel with the party in power. Influential men on both sides are cultivated; free passes are a usual attention to prominent men; editors and legislators all travel on free passes; members of Congress and senators of the United States are favourites; many are avowedly elected in that interest; others, who belong to the legal profession, are retained professionally; influence is brought to bear in a hundred ways which are not directly dishonourable, and, when necessary, the purchasing power of money is freely used. In the report of a committee appointed by the Legislature of the State of New York, in 1872, to investigate the affairs of the Erie railroad, we find the following :—

" It is further in evidence that it has been the custom of the managers of the Erie railway, from year to year in the past, to spend large sums to control elections and to influence legislation. In the year 1868 more than 1,000,000 dollars was disbursed from the treasury for ' extra and legal service.' "

It is admitted that the elections of 1874 carried into office a very large number of " railroad men," and it is said that a representative of one of the trunk lines—in commenting upon this fact —recently observed that they would " control the next ' presidential election.' "

Certainly this looks as if the prophecy before noted, that it was " destined to become the dominant interest in the United States," is likely to be soon fulfilled.

So much for steam and electricity in their commercial and political bearings. Now let us examine into their

Economical Features.

It is generally admitted that all material wealth is the product of labour. From time immemorial those who have controlled the greatest amount of reliable and intelligent labour have also accumu-

16

lated the greatest wealth and possessed the greatest power. Steam is the greatest saver of labour ; or, more correctly, performs the greatest amount of labour, and is therefore the greatest creator of wealth in existence. Within forty years it has quadrupled the producing capacity of all civilized nations; nay, it has done even more, it has created wants for the purpose of consuming its over-abundance of supply; furnishing as it does an unlimited supply of cheap, reliable, and never-tiring power, it has stimulated the brain of the inventor to produce cunning methods of applying it ; and machinery with its thousand and one combinations produce results which, in massiveness or delicacy, far outstrip the possi-bilities of human labour. No combination of human muscle can drive a mighty ship across the ocean in eight days, or an express train at the rate of forty miles an hour ; yet these have become matters of every day life ; and as this great power is supplemented by its active co-worker, electricity, which is soon destined to veritably " put a girdle round the earth in forty minutes," what may we not expect in the way of material progress during the next forty years ? .

To realise, however, the benefits of these great factors in modern civilization, they must not be monopolised by any one class to the exclusion of others. Like light, or air, or water, they are God's gifts to the human race, and should be possessed and enjoyed by every one. Thus far, however, they have been largely monopolised by the moneyed classes, because they have possessed the means of applying them to the wants of the human family. The great middle class has been charged exorbitantly for their use, and the labouring classes have benefited but little by their discovery.

This cannot go on for ever without subverting the principles upon which our government is founded ; it lies at the root of the question of the relations of capital and labour—at the root of every strike and every lock-out.

The wise men who framed the constitution of the United States knew the selfishness of human nature, and provided for the protection of the weak against the strong ; they knew the power and tempta-tion of great aggregations of wealth in the hands of a few, and the benefit of a diffusion of it in the hands of the many ; hence they at one stroke abolished the law of primogeniture—a law which for centuries had been one of the features of government in the prin-cipal nations of the earth. But they could not foresee that these agencies would enable capitalists to control the transportation system of a continent, and by taxing every producer and consumer in the land, accumulate in a day fortunes which formerly required the toil of a series of generations. They did not deem it possible for a few individuals to acquire the power to buy up the gold of a nation, and compel every legitimate trader to pay exorbitantly for its use ; and that to perpetuate their power, they would seek to control, either by ownership or patronage, "the press," that bulwark of our free institutions. If they could have foreseen these results, can there be a doubt that they would have endeavoured to provide against them ?

One of the things to be done is to educate the lower classes and qualify them for a higher citizenship; teach them to read and to write, so that they may learn the duties of a citizen.

The middle and higher classes in this country also need education—education in their duties as citizens. Many a man does not prize highly enough his right as a citizen to go to the polls and vote, or having voted, he considers that his whole duty is performed ; he knows men for whom he would prefer to vote, but cannot, because he, and his like, failed to attend the primary meetings at which the question of nominations is virtually decided ; so an inferior or unworthy man is nominated and elected to make laws for the community which he is unfit to represent.

When these facts are presented to busy men, they will tell you that they "have no time to attend to politics ; " but this can never be a valid excuse. Every citizen *must*, to some extent, attend to politics, or the Republic in time will be subverted. There is an alarming amount of carelessness and indifference among the better classes in regard to exercising the right of franchise.

They are apparently so absorbed in the rush and hurry of the age—so engrossed with the cares of business—so intent upon the things which press more immediately upon their attention, that they neglect more important things, which are only a little more remote.

The producing and mercantile classes are suffering at this time because they have had no voice in the legislation of the forty years last past ; all that time they have been electing lawyers and professional politicians to office, some of whom were dishonest, and most of whom cared more for the intrigues of party than for the material welfare of their country. Instead of attempting to solve the great questions of the day, statesmanship seems to consist of attempts to prove the one party worse than the other.

But these questions are even now pressing upon us. · Steam and electricity are driving us forward at a tremendous pace ; each ten years the census reveals facts which make us almost doubt the evidence of our senses.

Novel and ingenious applications of steam and electricity are so frequent that they now scarcely excite more than a passing remark ; but when we look back upon the progress made in each decade, we realise the truth that there may be in the song of steam :—

> " I've no muscle to weary, no breast to decay,
>   No bones to be laid on the shelf;
> And soon I intend you may go and play,
>   While I manage the world myself."

These lines were written in 1848 by George W. Cutter, and were then considered in the highest degree fanciful and unreal; but in the light of the progress of only twenty-seven years it seems—like Shakespeare's promise to "put a girdle round the earth in forty minutes"—almost prophetic.—*Thurber on Electricity and Steam.*

The reader will no longer object to these lengthy extracts from American writers, when he takes into consideration that the threat to resort to gold payments in 1878 is exciting the most intense interest in that country, now suffering the utmost extremity of distress from the mere anticipation. This is evidenced by the issue of numerous pamphlets (one of which is given below), and by the bitter controversies and angry discussions carried on in newspapers; this is especially the case in the Western States, where men who have studied the question, and mastered the first principles of the Science of Money, are actively engaged in instructing the people. It must be borne in mind too that we have Professor Bonamy Price's assurance (p. 5), "that the advocacy of Paper Money has wholly disappeared from English literature," so that, excepting John Ruskin, there is not with us a living writer of any note to be appealed to, or quoted.

APPENDIX V.

Mr. WILLIAM BROWN OF MONTREAL—"THOUGHTS ON PAPER CURRENCY AND LENDING ON INTEREST."

MR. BROWN in denouncing paper currency, does not mean the paper money issued by the States, but the "I promise to pay" notes of bankers, etc. He concludes by the following eloquent peroration:—

"Our youthful country [Canada], under wise counsels, may be made great and prosperous, but never under the growing burden of a national debt, and its close ally, a paper currency.* A national debt, for whatever purpose incurred, is only second in its evils to a paper currency. It is a source of feverish excitement and of much corruption to a nation, tending to reduce all labour to a state of bondage, and introducing two hostile elements in the persons of the few who hold the debt and the many who have to pay it, and in addition demoralizing society by the facilities it opens up for gambling on the most extensive scale. The stock and share markets, lawful and honourable

* The paper here objected to is the certificate of gold: the bank note "promising to pay" gold.

in themselves, and under *a money system*, a secure place of investment for the savings of industry and for the support of old age, become, under the *no money system*, a field where the worst characters can play their desperate game. Is there really any moral obligation resting at this moment on the working men of Great Britain to pay the interest of a debt contracted by the aristocracy of past generations for the purpose of carrying on continental wars? Is there really any obligation on labour that it should pay for all this blood-shedding and ruin?—that the ploughshare and the pruning-hook should be for ever compelled to pay for the devastation wrought by the sword and the spear? We have the happiness or misery of many millions in our hands, and are, to a large extent, the trustees of the independence and prosperity of future generations. On our own heads will be the guilt of the wrong doing, if we leave to this young nation only an inheritance of debt and mortgage to eat as a canker into the lifeblood of those who come after us, and to embitter all their toil.

" Hardly a merchant but has suffered the deepest mental agony and distress through his connection with it. Business itself is a pleasure, but it is the anxieties and burdens of business arising all out of this debt system, which has caused so many aching pillows and so many broken hearts. What countless multitudes, during the last three hundred years, have gone down to bankruptcy and shame—what fair prospects have been for ever blighted—what happy homes desolated—what peace destroyed—what ruin and destruction have ever marched hand in hand with this system of debt, paper, and usury. Verily its sins have reached unto heaven, and its iniquities are very great.

" What shall the end of these things be? God only knoweth. I fear the system is beyond a cure. All the great interests of humanity are overborne by it, and nothing can flourish as it ought till it is taken out of the way. It contains within itself, as we have at times witnessed, most potent elements of destruction which in one hour may bring all its riches to nought. It seems as if, in the providence of God, it required but a national debt to settle down upon the American people, to bring all the traffic of civilized lands within the reach of these destructive forces ; and there is, in the debt currency of all the nations, enough of inflammable material for the final conflagration. What if we are drawing near that period of stupendous interest in the world's history !

" Usury, and its concomitant, debt, affect all the daily transactions of life, have entered into every household, and have permeated into every rank and condition of society, and have thus reared up an obstacle to the progress of Christianity so vast and powerful that it seems as if its ultimate destruction were beyond the reach of human instrumentality.

" The blood of millions ' slain upon the earth ' is in her skirts, and a terrible reckoning will doubtless be made for that blood through the collapse and ruin of the debts of the nations, incurred, as they have been, for the destruction of life and of the fruits of industry. · The system stands on a foundation of sand, and holds its vast wealth, with all its public and national debts, by a most frail tenure; and it needs but the breath of suspicion to fan its own slumbering fires into a sea of flame so devastating and fierce that everything within it shall be utterly consumed. At the present day it sits as a queen, and says in its heart that it shall see no sorrow. Other systems of error have crumbled into dissolution by the gradual entrance of light and truth, but this has wrested the great economic laws of nature to its own destruction, and will make no surrender of its pretensions till overthrown, as in a moment by divine power. It will come to a violent end, and will disappear as thoroughly from the face of the earth as the great millstone flung from the angel's hand. It has corrupted the commerce of the whole earth, it has placed its brand upon every product of man's industry, and literally none can now buy and sell without its mark and the number of its name. All the world wonders after it, and its deluded worshippers conceive of no termination to its reign. But its doom is written. The day of its final and terrible destruction draweth nigh, and its sceptre shall depart for ever. Heaven itself will then rejoice over its sudden and tremendous fall. Then shall LABOUR lift its head, and INDUSTRY be glad, and TOIL have its holiday, and WORK be free, and COMMERCE be wholly sanctified to the Lord. Then shall the earth yield her increase, and God, even our own God, shall bless us. Then, and not till then, shall the golden age of the world begin."—" *Thoughts on Paper Money and Lending at Interest.*"

APPENDIX W.

MOSAIC MANUFACTURE IN FLORENCE.

THE immense wealth of the Florentine bankers prompted them to indulge in all that fantastic and childish expenditure which a sickly and depraved taste dictates.

Like the Chinese Mandarin who indulges in elaborate carving in ivory, and even on plum-stones, he takes advantage of cheap labour to consign his poorer countrymen to the dreadful and debasing drudgery of consuming life in the elaborate production of what he feels, as he slaves, to be useless toys. This waste of that most sacred of all things, labour, is going on to a great extent in this country, and is defended by even political economists, on the plea of providing employment.

The most striking misapplication of labour is the working in mosaics, a Florentine speciality, thus described by Mark Twain:

"Magnanimous Florence! her jewellery marts are filled with artists in mosaic. Florentine mosaics are the choicest in the world; Florence loves to have that said; Florence is proud of it; Florence would foster this speciality of hers. She is grateful to the artists that bring to her this high credit, and fill her coffers with foreign money, and so she encourages them with pensions. With pensions! Think of the lavishness of it. She knows that people who piece together these beautiful trifles die early, because the labour is so confining and so exhausting to hand and brain, and so she has decreed that all these people who reach the age of sixty shall have a pension. I have not heard that any of them have called for their dividends yet. One man did fight along until he was sixty, and started after his pension; but it appeared that there had been a mistake of a year in his family records, so he gave it up, and died.

"These artists will take particles of stone and glass, no larger than a mustard seed, and piece them together on a sleeve, or on a shirt stud so smoothly, and with such nice adjustment of the delicate shades of colour the pieces bear, as to form a pigmy rose, with stem, thorns, leaves, and petals complete, and all as softly and as truthfully tinted as though nature had builded it herself. They will counterfeit a fly, or a high-toned bug, or the ruined Coliseum within the cramped circle of a breastpin, and so deftly and so neatly that any man might think a master had painted it. I saw a little table in the great mosaic school in Florence, a little trifle of a centre-table, whose top was made of some sort of precious polished stone, and in the stone was inlaid the figure of a flute, with bell mouth, and mazy complication of keys. No painting in the world could have been softer or richer; no shading out of one tint into another could have been more perfect; no work of art of any kind could have been more faultless than this flute; and yet, to count the multitude of little fragments of stone, of which they swore it was formed, would bankrupt any man's arithmetic.

"I do not think one could have seen where two particles joined each other with eyes of ordinary shrewdness. Certainly we could detect no such blemish. This table top cost the labour of one man for ten long years, so they said, and it was for sale for thirty-five thousand dollars."—*Mark Twain's "Innocents Abroad."*